Public Wrongs, Private Actions

Public Wrongs, Private Actions

Civil Lawsuits to Recover Stolen Assets

Jean-Pierre Brun
Pascale Helene Dubois
Emile van der Does de Willebois
Jeanne Hauch
Sarah Jaïs
Yannis Mekki
Anastasia Sotiropoulou
Katherine Rose Sylvester
Mahesh Uttamchandani

StAR — Stolen Asset Recovery Initiative

The World Bank • UNODC

ISBN (paper): 978-1-4648-0370-3
ISBN (electronic): 978-1-4648-0373-4
DOI: 10.1596/978-1-4648-0370-3

Cover photos: shutterstock.com. Reuse requires permission.
Cover design: Debra Naylor, Naylor Design, Inc.

Library of Congress Cataloging-in-Publication Data has been applied for.

Contents

Figures

Tables

Preface

Over the last decade, and particularly since the entry into force of the United Nations Convention Against Corruption, corruption and the recovery of stolen assets have steadily become more prominent in the international policy agenda. This book studies how states may bring private civil lawsuits to recover stolen assets and how civil remedies can usefully complement criminal and administrative avenues.

There are four main avenues through which states may pursue asset recovery: criminal prosecution and confiscation, non-conviction-based (NCB) confiscation, administrative confiscation, and private lawsuits based on civil remedies.

Criminal prosecution and confiscation. Asset recovery by way of a criminal conviction and confiscation acts as a deterrent to future criminal conduct and provides a wide array of coercive procedural measures at the disposal of enforcement authorities to conduct their investigation. That said, criminal proceedings also come with some limitations. These include, among others, a high standard of proof for criminal convictions and often very slow mutual legal assistance processes in the context of multijurisdictional investigations. Moreover, criminal prosecution may be ineffective in the case of the death of the defendant, or if he has fled the jurisdiction or has immunities.

To date, the amounts of money recovered in the context of criminal cases are still relatively modest when compared with the scale of the thefts. To compensate these challenges, jurisdictions have developed other options, including NCB or administrative confiscation.

NCB confiscation requires proof that the property is the proceeds or an instrumentality of crime. However, the standard of proof for NCB will often be on a "balance of probabilities," which means that the state may obtain civil forfeiture even when there is insufficient evidence to support a criminal conviction.

Administrative confiscation without judicial action may also be used in some jurisdictions to freeze and confiscate assets through executive or parliamentary order.

NCB and administrative confiscations, however, are not available, workable, or recognized in all jurisdictions, which brings its own challenges in terms of international asset recovery. Other innovative methods to recover stolen assets, along with developments in public policy, can help change that situation. Civil lawsuits are one of them.

Civil lawsuits. Authorities seeking to recover stolen assets have the option of initiating proceedings in domestic or foreign civil courts to secure and recover the assets. They may seek damages based on torts, breach of contract, illicit enrichment, or other theories. Such a lawsuit is a civil action between two private persons in the courts of law, by which a plaintiff who claims to have incurred loss as a result of a defendant's actions requests a legal or equitable remedy. Although there are pluses and minuses to civil remedies, on balance they are clearly worthy of consideration.

First, in a civil trial, the standards of proof are often lower than in criminal proceedings. For example, common law countries often allow the claimant to prove the civil case by using a "balance of probabilities," that is, that a fact is more likely than not.

Second, the possibility of bringing a claim for general damages in a civil suit overcomes some proof problems where the link between the asset and the misconduct is weak by criminal standards. Where establishing a direct link between the corruption and the asset is impossible, a civil claim may still have chances of success.

Third, in some jurisdictions, criminal liability may not extend to corporations and other legal entities, and only individuals are subject to criminal prosecutions. In that context, civil remedies and private lawsuits appear as a powerful instrument for governments in their efforts to recover the proceeds of corruption.

Finally, private lawsuits and civil remedies may extend the scope of potential defendants and liabilities, meaning "deeper pockets" to sue and more of them. An injured party may seek to bring a civil action, claiming damages from third parties. These third parties could include anyone who knowingly assisted the main actor, such as family members and associates, lawyers, banks, and bankers. Importantly, in the context of civil lawsuits, officials or former officials and their assets may not enjoy the same kind of immunity as in the context of criminal prosecutions.[1]

The study proceeds through the various topics and steps for states to consider when contemplating civil action in foreign courts. To this end, it describes the various strategic, tactical, and technical issues of the legal action and discusses answers to very practical issues:

- Who may sue and be sued
- How or where to file a case
- How to select and pay lawyers
- What kinds of legal actions or claims are available
- How to collect evidence and secure assets
- How to use international instruments

---

1. See, for example, the StAR study *Barriers to Asset Recovery* (Washington, DC: World Bank, 2011), 71–74.

- How to estimate amounts to recover
- How to enforce and collect judgments in another country
- How can insolvency and receivership processes be used to trace and recover assets

We hope that the book, designed as a how-to manual, will prove useful as a quick reference for policy makers and practitioners contemplating private lawsuits in asset recovery cases. We look forward to continuing to provide technical assistance and capacity building in countries interested in the StAR initiative.

Acknowledgments

This study is the result of special collaborative efforts from colleagues around the world. Their time and expertise were invaluable in developing a practical tool to assist practitioners in using private lawsuits and civil remedies to recover the proceeds and instrumentalities of corruption.

This publication was written by Jean-Pierre Brun (World Bank and StAR, Task Team Leader), Pascale Dubois (Chief Suspension and Debarment Officer, World Bank), Emile van der Does de Willebois (World Bank and StAR), Jeanne Hauch (World Bank and StAR), Anastasia Sotiropoulou (Lawyer, Instructor of Criminology, American College of Greece), Sarah Jaïs (Consultant, World Bank and StAR), Yannis Mekki (World Bank and StAR), Katherine Rose Sylvester (Consultant, Office of Suspension and Debarment, World Bank), and Mahesh Uttamchandani (Lead Private Sector Development Specialist, World Bank). Angana R. Shah (Consultant, World Bank) contributed to the drafting of chapter 9.

The authors are especially grateful to Jean Pesme (Manager, Financial Market Integrity Unit and StAR coordinator) for his ongoing support and guidance on this project.

The team benefited from many insightful comments during the peer review process, which was chaired by Jean Pesme (Manager, Financial Market Integrity Unit and StAR coordinator).

The peer reviewers were Lisa Bostwick (World Bank, FPDFI, and StAR), Franck Fariello (World Bank, Legal Vice Presidency), Yves Klein (Switzerland, Monfrini Crettol & Partners), Erik Larson (U.S. State Department), Olaf Meyer (Germany, University of Bremen), Boni de Moraes Soares (Brazil, State Attorney), and Susan Rose-Ackerman (United States, Yale Law School).

As part of the drafting and consultation process, practitioners were consulted and brought experience in conducting civil actions and international cooperation processes in both civil and common law jurisdictions. The contributors were Edward Davies (Astigarraga Davis), Stephane Bonifassi (Lebray & Associés), and Yves Klein (Switzerland, Monfrini Crettol & Partners).

Introduction

"Bribery is an evil practice which threatens the foundations of any civilized society."
Lord Templeman Justice Longmore, in Attorney General
for *Hong Kong v. Reid* [1]

Corruption is the abuse of power for personal gain. When perpetrated by public officials, these abuses are public wrongs, as defined by William Blackstone as "breaches and violations of duties due to the whole community, considered as a community, in its social aggregate capacity."[2] Corruption and thefts of public assets harm a diffuse set of victims, weaken confidence in public institutions, damage the private investment climate, and threaten the foundations of the society as a whole. In addition, in developing countries with scarce public resources, the cost of corruption is an impediment to development: developing countries lose between US$20 billion to US$40 billion each year through bribery, misappropriation of funds, and other corrupt practices.[3] Each of these criminal acts includes an injury: corruption is by no means a "victimless crime." Hence, the wrongful depletion of public resources—a public wrong—may also cause particular and personal harms to states' and government entities' interests. This book aims to explore the standing of states and government entities as those harmed by corruption and then explains how they can act as private litigants and bring civil suits to recover assets lost to corruption.

Over the last decade, corruption and the recovery of stolen assets have steadily risen in the international policy agenda, starting with the entry into force of the United Nations Convention Against Corruption (UNCAC) in 2005, through the Arab Spring in 2011, and most recently a string of scandals in the financial sector. Corruption diverts resources from development and reduces the potential for economic growth. The G20 and many regional and civil society organizations have all put forward ideas on how best to tackle corruption, ranging from promoting preventive measures, to fostering international cooperation, and initiating more vigorous criminal proceedings.

As states decide how best to respond to corruption and recover assets, the course of action most often discussed is criminal investigation and prosecution, as opposed to private lawsuits. Indeed, when confronted with abuse of power, the first response is often to initiate enforcement action against the wrongdoer, typically by aiming for

---

1. Attorney General for Hong Kong v. Reid [1994] 1 Ac 324 at 330-1.
2. William Blackstone, *Commentaries of the Laws of England, bk. 4, ch. 1, Of the Nature of Crimes; and Their Punishment*, Oxford University Press, 1765–69.
3. *Stolen Asset Recovery (StAR) Initiative: Challenges, Opportunities, and Action Plan* (Washington, DC: World Bank, 2007).

a prison term combined with the confiscation of the profits gained by the corrupt actor. This effort may fall short.

Moreover, the criminal response frequently fails to capture an important component of the effects of corruption. Certainly the transgressor must be held criminally and personally accountable for the harm he caused to society as a whole. Yet corruption causes tangible damages to particular categories of persons as well. Without doubt, those persons, be they natural or legal, as well as the governments, are entitled to recover lost assets and/or receive compensation for the damage suffered. While providing for a direct and efficient way to compensate victims for the harm they have suffered, private lawsuits could also prove valuable to deter future corrupt actions by depriving the corrupt actors of their ill-gotten gains and thus frustrate the goal underlying most criminal conduct. To accomplish the goals of recovery and compensation, private or "civil" actions are often a necessary and useful complement to criminal proceedings. Furthermore, such civil actions can persist when the criminal action is at a dead end. This study focuses on how state victims of corruption can use these civil legal remedies as a private claimant to recover assets.

Objective

The goal of this work is to promote knowledge and understanding, as well as increase the use of civil remedies and private lawsuits to recover stolen assets in the context of UNCAC offenses. UNCAC, the global standard for the fight against corruption, does not contain a legal definition of "corruption" itself but lists an array of offenses, including public and private sector bribery and the embezzlement of public and private sector funds. The book mainly focuses on these types of corruption, namely, bribery, embezzlement of funds, and other UNCAC offenses.

This study is not intended in any way to minimize the importance of criminal proceedings and confiscation in addressing acts of corruption. Rather, it shows that civil law remedies can effectively complement criminal penalties by attacking the economic base of corrupt activities in both the public and the private sectors. In fact, given the magnitude of the challenges, all avenues of asset recovery, be they criminal or civil, should be explored simultaneously to tackle corruption from every angle and achieve the goals of deterrence and enforcement. While criminal law expresses society's disapproval of the corrupt acts and aims at dissuasion, punishment, and confiscation of illicit proceeds, civil law focuses on victims' interests and aims at compensation and restitution. These procedures occur sometimes in parallel, sometimes sequentially. Thus, an effective response to corruption will usually require concomitant use of both criminal and civil law remedies to achieve the desired result.[4]

---

4. James Maton and Tim Daniel, "Recovering the Proceeds of Corruption by Public Officials: A Case-Study," *ERA Forum* 10 (2009): 453, 463.

Context: Civil Remedies as One of Several Avenues to Asset Recovery

To place civil remedies in context, they are one of four avenues through which states may pursue asset recovery, as detailed below. The first, the criminal route, is familiar to all. The book also defines two others—non-conviction based confiscation and administrative confiscation, before returning to the focus on civil lawsuits.

Criminal Prosecution and Confiscation. First, the home country of the allegedly corrupt official or agent, or a country in which proceeds of corruption are found, may seek to recover stolen assets by pursuing a criminal case. Following the criminal route, the state must obtain a conviction, and then it can seek to confiscate the proceeds of crime, either domestically or internationally. Indeed, an order for criminal confiscation can be obtained only after a criminal conviction or guilty plea.

In common law jurisdictions, the standard of proof in a criminal trial is "beyond a reasonable doubt," and in civil law ones by "intimate conviction." Once the standard is met and a conviction obtained, the prosecution must then show that the assets are "proceeds" of the crime of which the defendant was convicted. The legal standard for proving that an asset constitutes the proceeds of a crime may be lower than "beyond a reasonable doubt." The standard may be the "balance of probabilities"—implying that it is more probable than not that the assets in question derived from criminal activity.

If those assets are located in another country, the authorities in the prosecuting country will need to request mutual legal assistance from the country where the assets are located. It may ask the other country either (a) to recognize the confiscation order directly or execute the order, or (b) to initiate its own proceedings to determine the illicit provenance of the proceeds and, following that country's own legal process, repatriate the assets back to the country that initiated the original criminal trial.

Asset recovery by way of a criminal conviction and confiscation offers various advantages. Criminal punishments (be they monetary sanctions or prison sentences) act as a deterrent to future criminal conduct. In addition, the criminal route provides a wide array of coercive procedural measures at the disposal of enforcement authorities to conduct their investigation. But criminal proceedings come with some limitations as well. They include, among others, a high standard of proof for criminal convictions and the expense in terms of resources and time-consuming, multijurisdictional investigations. Moreover, criminal prosecution is not effective in cases of the death of the defendant, or if he has fled the jurisdiction or has immunities.

Non-conviction Based Confiscation. Second, in some jurisdictions, the state may obtain a confiscation order without a conviction, also known as "non-conviction based" confiscations or "civil forfeiture" or "civil recovery." In addition to the main distinction between criminal forfeiture and civil forfeiture, that is, that criminal forfeiture requires a criminal trial and conviction, whereas civil forfeiture does not, a number of procedural differences are evident as well. Whereas criminal forfeiture is an *in personam* order, civil forfeiture is an *in rem* forfeiture order, meaning that the action is against the asset itself. Civil forfeiture is an action separate from any criminal proceeding and requires proof that the property be the proceeds or an instrumentality of crime. The standard of proof for such a confiscation will generally be a "balance of probabilities," that is to say, a less-demanding standard than the criminal standard. This means that it may be possible for the state to obtain civil forfeiture when there is insufficient evidence to support a criminal conviction. Non-conviction based confiscations are not available in all jurisdictions. When they exist, they are civil actions by the state in its sovereign capacity and as a result are brought before civil courts and follow the rules of civil procedures.[5]

Administrative Confiscation. Third, states may use various administrative remedies, including administrative confiscation without judicial action, freezes of assets through executive or parliamentary order, or administrative enforcement in court followed by confiscation orders. Unlike criminal or non-conviction based confiscation, in many legal systems administrative confiscation does not involve any criminal conviction, court proceedings, or even a judicial determination, but provides a nonjudicial mechanism for confiscating assets. It may occur by operation of statute or pursuant to procedures set out in regulations. It is often used to address uncontested confiscation cases. In certain legal systems, administrative law is used as the primary mechanism to enforce anti-bribery provisions and may result in large monetary penalties.[6]

Civil Lawsuits. Last, authorities seeking to recover stolen assets have the option of initiating proceedings in domestic or foreign civil courts to secure and recover the assets. They may seek damages based on torts, breach of contract, illicit enrichment, or other theories. A lawsuit is a civil action between two private persons in the courts of law, by which a plaintiff who claims to have incurred loss as a result of a defendant's actions requests a legal or equitable remedy. The courts of the foreign jurisdiction may be competent in any of the following situations: if a defendant is a person (individual or business entity) living or incorporated in the jurisdiction (personal jurisdiction); if the assets are within or have transited the jurisdiction (subject matter jurisdiction); or if an act of corruption or money laundering was committed within the jurisdiction.

---

5. For a more detailed analysis on non-conviction based forfeiture, please refer to Theodore S. Greenberg, Linda M. Samuel, Wingate Grant, and Larissa Gray, *A Good Practices Guide for Non-conviction Based Asset Forfeiture* (Washington, DC: World Bank, 2009).

6. Germany is an example of a jurisdiction having successful recourse to "administrative law" to enforce antibribery laws and confiscate assets. In Siemens Telecom and Other Sectors Cases (decision of the German Regional Court [Landgericht] of Munich I, October 4, 2007; decision of Public Prosecution Office Munich I in proceedings regarding an administrative offense, December 15, 2008), for example, administrative fines were imposed against Siemens in Germany for paying bribes in a number of countries to win contracts. Similarly, newer legislation in Switzerland and Tunisia provides for significant confiscation through administrative measures; see the Swiss Federal Act on the Restitution of Assets of Politically Exposed Persons Obtained by Unlawful Means (RIAA), which provides for administrative confiscation, and the Tunisian Decree-law Number 2011-13, dated March 14, 2011 (in French, the Decret-loi No 2011-13 mars 2011 *portant confiscation d'avoirs et de biens meubles et immeubles*). The Tunisian decree permitted the confiscation of billions of dollars of assets in the weeks following the end of the Ben-Ali regime. The decree is available at http://karari.org/fr/node/9641 (unofficial English translation of the decree).

There are pluses and minuses to civil remedies, but on balance, they are worthy of consideration. The principal disadvantages of litigating in a foreign jurisdiction are the challenges and cost of tracing assets without the benefit of investigative tools provided by criminal procedures and the high cost of litigation. However, the litigant may have more control in pursuing civil proceedings and assets in the hands of third parties. In addition, private lawsuits and civil remedies offer a number of advantages not available with the other remedies. Some of the main advantages of civil claims include less-demanding requirements for linking the assets to the wrongdoing, the ability to claim damages generally, rather than claim particular assets, and a wider choice of parties to sue.

First, civil lawsuits are often especially useful to address the financial consequences of corruption in cases where several corrupt acts have been committed over a longer period of time. Even if some or all of the acts of corruption are proven at a criminal trial, it may be nearly impossible to trace all proceeds because the "paper trail" is incomplete. If the direct link between the specific crime and the assets cannot be established, in many jurisdictions further criminal action and confiscation will be much more difficult. In some jurisdictions, the highest procedural guarantees and standards of proof, which apply in a criminal trial, may become impossible to meet. In contrast, in a civil trial, the standards of proof are often lower. For example, common law countries often allow the claimant to prove the case by using a "balance of probabilities," that is, that a fact is more likely than not. The state may be able to meet this lower standard of proof.

Second, the possibility of bringing a claim for general damages in a civil suit overcomes some proof problems in situations in which the link between the asset and the misconduct is weak. Where establishing a direct link between the corruption and the asset is impossible, a civil claim may still have chances of success. Large proportions of corruption proceeds are spent far from the country from which they were stolen. Purchasers may launder funds through many transactions, finally buying real estate, investing in businesses, or purchasing luxury items. In a jurisdiction where only the assets directly related to the crime can be confiscated, the items purchased with the tainted funds cannot be criminally confiscated. The problem will be more acute in jurisdictions that recognize only property-based confiscation (an action to recover a particular asset) and less so where value-based confiscation is permitted (a legal action to recover the value of benefits that have been derived from criminal conduct and the imposition of a monetary penalty of an equivalent value). In any case, civil proceedings can provide a remedy to this problem by establishing a general claim for damages.

Third, in some jurisdictions criminal liability may not extend to corporations and other legal entities, and only individuals are subject to criminal prosecutions. In that context, civil remedies and private lawsuits appear as a powerful instrument for governments in their efforts to recover the proceeds of corruption.

Finally, private lawsuits and civil remedies may extend the scope of potential defendants and liabilities, meaning "deeper pockets" to sue and more of them. An injured party may seek to bring a civil action claiming damages from third parties with substantial financial assets, whose forfeitable criminal gains may be negligible, or whose criminal liability cannot be proved beyond a reasonable doubt but can be proved under a lesser standard. Those third parties could include anyone who knowingly assisted the main actor, such as family members and associates, lawyers, banks, and bankers. If a third party acted in concert with other wrongdoers, he may be held liable for the greater damages caused by the others.[7] It is important to note that in the context of civil lawsuits officials or former officials and their assets may not enjoy the same kind of immunity as in the context of criminal prosecutions.[8]

Scope of the Book

The book focuses on states and government entities as private parties exercising a private right of action to seek relief for the harm caused to their financial interests.

States and related government entities have the right to act as private litigants (as any other plaintiff) to bring lawsuits to recover assets lost through corruption. States may bring private lawsuits to obtain compensation for damages caused by corruption, to obtain contractual restitutions, and in some cases to recover illicit profits or unjust enrichment.

The topic of this study is distinct from the context in which the state uses civil courts as an enforcer of its own laws. For example, agencies such as the U.S. Securities and Exchange Commission may rely on civil actions to resolve enforcement matters related to foreign bribery cases. However, the Foreign Corrupt Practices Act (FCPA) does not provide for a private right of action to seek disgorgement of illicit profits. Although these government agencies use civil remedies, they act as sovereign enforcers rather than civil parties.

Similarly, the topic of the study is distinguishable from non-conviction based confiscations (NCB), albeit civil remedies in nature but still retaining something of a criminal flavor. NCBs are civil remedies in the sense that they do not require criminal convictions, are brought before civil courts, and follow the rules of civil procedures. However, they relate to the proceeds of crime, that is, assets derived from criminal or unlawful conduct. Judicial complaints can be filed only by authorized enforcers, such as prosecutors or specialized agencies (asset recovery or anticorruption commissions). In addition, the evidence comes from police investigations, and the criminal conduct must be established to show that the targeted property is tainted. As a result, states usually pursue non-conviction based confiscations in a sovereign capacity and not as a mere private litigant.

---

7. This theory is sometimes known as "joint and several" liability, or in French, "*responsibilité solidaire*," meaning that one can sue any of the wrongdoers for all the harm caused, even if they personally did only a small part.

8. See, for example, Kevin M. Stephenson, Larissa Gray, Ric Power, Jean-Pierre Brun, Gabriele Dunker, and Melissa Panjer, *Barriers to Asset Recovery: An Analysis of the Key Barriers and Recommendations for Action* (Washington, DC: World Bank, 2011), 71–74.

The civil remedies used in enforcement actions are not the topic of this study. For more information on NCB or FCPA disgorgement procedures, the reader may consult other StAR publications that provide specific analysis.[9] However, some policies and practices related to these legal tools will be mentioned whenever they can help elucidate specific techniques that are also relevant for, or applicable to, private civil remedies.

Audience

This book aims to provide guidance to practitioners and policy makers around the world on how to combat corruption by using civil remedies and private lawsuits to recover stolen assets in the context of UNCAC offenses and their private civil law analogues. By identifying challenges, best practices, and case examples, the study intends to show that civil law remedies and private lawsuits are a credible and effective tool for countries to recover stolen assets. Civil remedies are especially effective when criminal law avenues either are unavailable or have a low likelihood of success.

Overview of Chapters

Chapter 1 focuses on who can sue and be sued—appropriate plaintiffs and defendants in a civil asset recovery

The injured state has a right to sue in other countries. International law assists in this respect, as the right of states to bring a private civil action in the courts in another state is recognized by UNCAC.[10] Each of the 171 parties to that treaty is bound to provide this right to other states.[11] As an alternative to filing a case in another country, states may also consider bringing a civil action in their own courts and seeking to enforce the decisions in the jurisdiction where the assets are located. In any case, determining who can be the plaintiff and the defendant in such lawsuits is of great importance. Typically claims may be brought against the corrupt actor, as well as against those who assisted him in stealing, concealing, or laundering the proceeds of the corrupt acts, and perhaps against intermediaries as well.

---

9. For more details, see Theodore S. Greenberg, Linda M. Samuel, Wingate Grant, and Larissa Gray, *A Good Practices Guide for Non-conviction Based Asset Forfeiture* (Washington, DC: World Bank, 2009); and the joint OECD-StAR analysis, *Identification and Quantification of the Proceeds of Bribery*, 2011, available on the Stolen Asset Recovery Initiative (StAR) website.

10. United Nations Convention Against Corruption, at Article 53 Paragraph (a), allows a foreign state party to initiate civil action. Paragraph (c) requires states to permit other states "to initiate civil action in [their] courts to establish title to or ownership of property acquired through the commission of an offence established in accordance with this Convention."

11. Other harmed persons might have a right to sue as well; see United Nations Convention Against Corruption at Article 35.

Chapters 2 discusses the relevant criteria and concrete steps for selection and engagement of lawyers

Once potential defendants and assets have been identified, the next step for the plaintiff will be to evaluate whether to bring a lawsuit and how and where to file a case, including the selection of lawyers. The processes regarding the hiring of legal counsel and choice of forum often arise simultaneously. Depending on the specific circumstances of the case, the selection of law firms can precede or follow the consideration of where to bring the lawsuit. Thus, this order of the chapters could just as easily be reversed. Litigation is a branch of law in which local expertise and experience in the courts where the claim is brought are essential. At the same time, an ideal lawyer also has experience in international asset recovery cases. Given the complexities of international asset recovery, one lawyer in one jurisdiction would rarely be sufficient to handle the case. States will need a multijurisdictional legal strategy, with various attorneys working as a coherent team. The chapter also discusses the crucial question of how much and how the attorneys should be paid—referred to as the "fee arrangement." Estimated total litigation costs must be weighed against what amounts may be recovered if the state prevails on its claims. There are often other considerations in assessing the opportunity to pursue a claim or not, such as the principle that no one should be able to profit from his own wrong.

Chapter 3 addresses the issue of where to bring a lawsuit

When considering where to sue, States should consider the location of the assets and the defendants, the types of legal claims and remedies in a particular jurisdiction, and how easy or difficult it would be to "enforce" a judgment if the state prevails on its claims. For example, if it is easy to get a judgment in country A, but the assets are located in country B, and the courts of country B are unlikely to enforce that judgment from country A, the state might want to consider bringing its claim in country B. Another criterion is whether a criminal action is already pending somewhere and what civil actions may be available in the jurisdiction where the criminal action is under way. Once the selection of counsel and venues has been considered, a state must identify (through consultation with the selected lawyers) the kinds of legal claims that are available to address the corrupt acts.

Chapter 4 discusses what claim to bring—the various types of civil actions

While the particular legal theories available will vary by country, certain types of claims should be considered. The two primary categories are "proprietary" and "personal." The first group involves the theory that the corrupt person has taken a particular asset that previously belonged to the state, or that is beneficially owned by the state, so that the state is merely reclaiming its own property. These are called "proprietary" claims and target particular assets. The second group of claims, called "personal" claims, generally involves actions against the corrupt person or third parties for monetary damages, rather than an action to reclaim a specific asset. For example, personal claims may include an action for breach of contract, for compensation through damages, or for recompense for unjust enrichment. In some civil law countries, restitution or compensation of damages can be claimed in the context of criminal prosecutions as the civil party (in French the *partie civile*), as well as in separate civil actions.

Chapter 5 explains how to investigate and freeze assets—the measures available to collect evidence and secure assets during lengthy civil litigation

Once claims have been identified and lawyers hired, the next step will be to collect evidence and, if possible, secure the assets that have been traced and identified. It is easier to secure specific assets if the party brings a "proprietary" claim concerning that asset. In all cases, it is critical to avoid dissipation or loss of value. Assets can move or change form with the click of a computer mouse. Quick action is essential.

Chapter 6 provides an overview of how to obtain evidence from abroad

As legal complaints are being filed and assets secured, the lawyers must collect evidence and provide a court with the evidence to support the claims. Often that evidence will be located in another country. Special methods exist to obtain that evidence, involving the use of international treaties.

Chapter 7 discusses how much to sue for—the methods of calculation that may be used

An important consideration when contemplating a civil case is the potential amount that may be recovered. What amount of money is a court likely to award? Even though there might be several considerations in deciding whether it is worth bringing a lawsuit or not, one of the most important elements to consider is whether the expected returns exceed the expected costs. A number of methods may be used to calculate that amount. The state will need to quantify the monetary consequences of corrupt conduct to justify the amount it claims in damages. In most countries, such as the United Kingdom, it is also possible to recover the legal fees and costs of successfully bringing proceedings against the defendant. (It is, however, a double-edged sword: if one loses, one must pay the fees of one's opponent.)

Chapter 8 reviews how to collect the assets—the various approaches to enforcing civil judgments

Assuming that the litigation is successful and a civil judgment is obtained against the corrupt defendant, unless the assets are located in the country in which the litigation was brought, the state will have to enforce that judgment in another country. "Enforcement" in this context means collecting any judgment against an asset held by the defendant up to the value stipulated in the judgment. As with the gathering of evidence, certain international treaties may be of use, particularly those that provide for recognition of judgments of other states parties. The bottom line is that a judgment is only useful if it can be enforced where the assets of the defendant are located.

Chapter 9 provides a brief preview of how to take advantage of insolvency and receivership proceedings in the context of asset recovery actions

Finally, although it is perhaps not obvious at first glance, failing corporate entities may offer opportunities for asset recovery. Insolvency and receivership processes can also be used to trace and recover assets. Because those proceedings are complex and technical in nature, they are very specific and beyond the scope of this general study; however, a preview will be provided.

These chapters as a whole provide an introduction to why and how states can use private civil lawsuits to recover assets. The utility of this study lies not in trying to explain exactly how and where to bring and pursue civil claims. A matter of such complexity must be left in the hands of capable experts, that is, the attorneys selected by the states. The expected value of the book lies in providing states with the basic considerations to bear in mind when deploying civil remedies to go after corruption. Civil remedies add another arrow to the quiver of tools available to target corruption and recover stolen assets.

1. Civil Asset Recovery Litigation: Who May Sue and Be Sued—States as Plaintiffs and Possible Defendants

States and a wide array of other parties may bring private legal actions in an attempt to recover assets. Victims of corruption are diverse and often go beyond the scope of potential plaintiffs who are able to assert a claim in the courts. In theory, any person, whether natural or legal, may be a victim of an act of corruption (bribery, embezzlement, misuse of corporate assets, etc.). In practice, the scope of potential claimants is limited to parties who have a specific legal interest in the case.

Although the present study concentrates on the claims of states or government entities seeking to recover stolen assets or receive compensation for damages caused by corruption, there are also other possible plaintiffs in civil asset recovery cases worth mention. They include, for example, an employer against his employee engaged in bribery or other fraudulent activity, leading to a loss for the company; rival bidders for contracts that lost a business deal due to a secret payment made by a competitor;[1] shareholders;[2] and civil society (citizens and nongovernmental organizations, or NGOs).[3] The schema in figure 1.1 illustrates who might be hurt by corruption understood in its widest form.

This study focuses on states and government entities acting as private litigants. This chapter will first discuss how states and relevant entities (the plaintiffs) may bring claims for asset recovery in civil courts (A) and then examine who can be sued (the defendants) (B).

---

1. See, for example, Korea Supply Co. v. Lockheed Martin Corp., 29 Cal. 4th 1134, 63 P.3d 937 (Cal. 2003). In this case, a competitor who did not win a contract because the winner paid bribes to Korean officials established a tort claim.
2. See, for example, SNC-Lavalin civil suits in Canada. The claims arise from alleged payments made by SNC-Lavalin to associates and agents of Libya's former Muammar Gaddafi regime to secure contracts for infrastructure projects in Libya. Judges in Ontario and Quebec certified shareholder class action lawsuits against SNC-Lavalin Group Inc. in September 2012 and January 2013. These actions seek damages based on the decline in market value of the securities purchased by the class members.
3. See, for example, in France, the participation of NGOs (Transparency International France, supported by SHERPA) as civil party in criminal proceedings in the case of the "Ill-gotten Gains" (*l'affaire des biens mal acquis*), *Cour de Cassation, Chambre criminelle*, November 9, 2010 (case n° 09-88272). See also In Re: Estate of Ferdinand E. Marcos Human Rights Litigation. Human Rights victims brought a class action against the estate of Ferdinand Marcos, the president of the Philippines from 1965 to 1986.

FIGURE 1.1   Corruption Harms Everybody

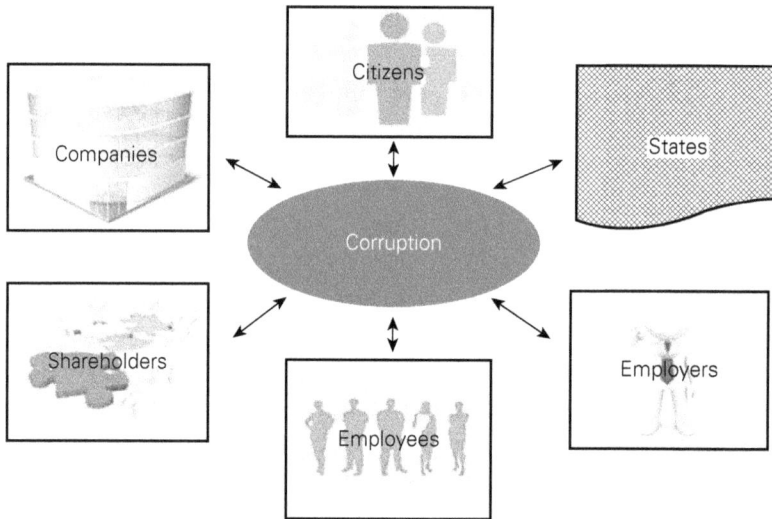

Source: World Bank.

A. States as Plaintiffs in Corruption Cases

Various international anticorruption instruments provide for the right of states to claim civil damages in corruption cases. In practice, the agencies empowered to bring such claims often include ministries, anticorruption agencies, and central banks. Other government entities, such as cities, provinces, and state-owned enterprises, may have legal rights to pursue claims. In some civil law jurisdictions, states and government entities may also participate in criminal proceedings as so-called civil party.[4]

1. International Legal Recognition of the Right to Sue

In most jurisdictions, the general rule is that any person or entity that has suffered loss as a result of corruption or entered into contracts tainted by corruption may bring a claim and an action for damages. Therefore authorities seeking to recover the proceeds of corruption often have the option to initiate civil proceedings in domestic or foreign civil courts in the same way as private citizens.

The United Nations Convention against Corruption (UNCAC) underlines the importance of civil proceedings and remedies in the fight against corruption. Indeed, Article 34 of the UNCAC stipulates that states parties may consider corruption as a relevant

---

4. The denominations vary depending on the jurisdictions. This action is also referred to as *partie civile* proceedings (or *action civile*) in France, Switzerland, and Belgium; *Acción Civil Resarcitoria* in Costa Rica; adhesion proceedings in Germany; or claims under property law in criminal proceedings in Central and Eastern Europe.

factor to declare transactions resulting from corrupt activities invalid, or may consider corruption as a factor to warrant rescinding contracts and withdrawing concessions.[5] Article 35 of the UNCAC requires state parties to take necessary measures and establish appropriate mechanisms to ensure that entities or persons who have suffered damage as a result of an act of corruption have the right to initiate legal action to obtain compensation.[6] Furthermore, Chapter V of the convention requires states parties to take measures to restrain, seize, confiscate, and return the proceeds of corruption, including civil proceedings and remedies. Article 53 Paragraph (a) of the UNCAC requires states to permit other states "to initiate civil action in (their) courts to establish title to or ownership of property acquired through the commission of an offense established in accordance with the Convention." In each jurisdiction, practitioners should review existing legislation to identify the laws that implement these provisions.

Likewise, regional recognition of the importance of civil proceedings to fight corruption has been attained through the Council of Europe Civil Law Convention. Article 1 of the Council of Europe Civil Law Convention on Corruption[7] requires state parties to enable "persons," natural or legal, who have suffered damage as a result of corruption to defend their rights and obtain damages.[8] Article 8§2 of the same convention also stipulates that "each Party shall provide in its internal law for the possibility for all parties to a contract whose consent has been undermined by an act of corruption to be able to apply to the court for the contract to be declared void, notwithstanding their claim for damages." The 35 countries that have ratified this convention are therefore bound to implement national legislation to enable a greater use of civil remedies by victims of corruption.[9]

---

5. UNCAC, Article 34, Consequences of acts of corruption: "With due regard to the rights of third parties acquired in good faith, each State Party shall take measures, in accordance with the fundamental principles of its domestic law, to address consequences of corruption. In this context, States Parties may consider corruption a relevant factor in legal proceedings to annul or rescind a contract, withdraw a concession or other similar instrument or take any other remedial action."

6. UNCAC, Article 35, Compensation for damage: "Each State Party shall take such measures as may be necessary, in accordance with principles of its domestic law, to ensure that entities or persons who have suffered damage as a result of an act of corruption have the right to initiate legal proceedings against those responsible for that damage in order to obtain compensation."

7. Civil Law Convention on Corruption, Nov. 4, 1999, Europ. T.S. No.174, http://conventions.coe.int/treaty /en/Treaties/Html/174.htm; Article 1 "Each Party shall provide in its internal law for effective remedies for persons who have suffered damage as a result of acts of corruption, to enable them to defend their rights and interests, including the possibility of obtaining compensation for damage."

8. Ibid. See also Civil Law Convention on Corruption, Explanatory Report paragraph 26, http://conventions .coe.int/Treaty/EN/Reports/Html/174.htm.

9. The Group of States against Corruption (GRECO) monitors the implementation of this convention by the Council of Europe States Parties and assesses regularly their legal framework. The importance of the use of civil remedies in the fight against corruption was recognized at the EU level as early as 1997 with the Twenty Guiding Principles for the Fight against Corruption, a directive adopted by the Committee of Ministers of the Council of Europe, which called upon its member states to "ensure that civil law takes into account the need to fight corruption and in particular provides for effective remedies for those whose rights and interests are affected by corruption" (Council of Europe, 1997, Principle 17).

2. Civil Proceedings Initiated by States and Other Government Entities

Many nations have recognized the right of foreign states to sue in their civil courts. Provisions on bringing a claim when the party has been harmed by corruption may be included in civil or criminal codes or in specific anticorruption legislation. For instance, in Kenya, the Anti-Corruption and Economic Crimes Act of 2003 (Part VI, Compensation and Recovery of Improper Benefits) provides in Article 51 that "[a] person who does anything that constitutes corruption or economic crime is liable to anyone who suffers a loss as a result for an amount that would be full compensation for the loss suffered." In the United States, under the Racketeering Influenced and Corrupt Organizations (RICO) statute, foreign governments or foreign nationals acting as civil plaintiffs may seek compensation for harm resulting from tortious corrupt practices.[10]

States may therefore file claims and receive civil compensation for damages caused by corruption, as described in box 1.1.

While legal standing is generally recognized for foreign state victims harmed in their proprietary interests, it may be denied under other circumstances when they do not have a specific and direct interest (see box 1.2).

An example of a successful civil case brought by a State before a foreign court and leading to recovery is the Nigerian case of Diepreye Alamieyeseigha, outlined in box 1.3.

The concept of public authorities covers not only states, but other public entities as well, such as municipalities, provinces, counties, and the like, and state-owned enterprises (SOEs).

Local public entities can also initiate civil proceedings when they demonstrate that they directly suffered from the wrongdoing of a former local leader. Box 1.4 illustrates the possibility for local entities to pursue civil proceedings in grand-scale corruption cases.

State-owned enterprises may also have an interest in initiating civil procedures as victims of fraudulent behavior. In common law systems, bribes paid to officers or agents of a company may be recovered by the company if the enterprise proves that the officer or agent had a fiduciary duty. The Pertamina case, described in box 1.5, is an example of a successful claim by a state-owned company.

3. States and Government Entities as Civil Party in Criminal Proceedings

In civil law jurisdictions, states and other government entities harmed by corruption may also have the opportunity to seek compensation through the criminal law system. In those jurisdictions, a state victim of a criminal offense may request civil party status within the criminal trial against the accused offender and, if granted, may participate as

---

10. RICO is a United States federal law enacted as section 901(a) of the Organized Crime Control Act of 1970 and can be found at Title 18 United States Code (U.S.C.) Section 1964.

| BOX 1.1 | States Are Legal Persons Entitled to Bring Claims: The Ferdinand Marcos Case (United States) |

The Republic of the Philippines filed a civil claim in the United States under the Racketeering Influenced and Corrupt Organizations (RICO) law alleging that its former president and his wife engaged in racketeering activity, committed numerous acts of mail/wire fraud, and transported stolen property in foreign or interstate commerce. The United States Court of Appeals for the Ninth Circuit held that the trial court had jurisdiction over the claim. According to the court, the foreign nature of the Republic of the Philippines did not deprive it of its status as a legal person for purposes of bringing a claim.

Note: Republic of the Philippines v. Marcos, 862 F.2d 1355 (9th Cir. 1988), *cert. denied*, 490 U.S. 1035 (1989).

| BOX 1.2 | Standing in Courts of Foreign States: *The Republic of Iraq v. ABB AG et al.* (United States) |

In 2008, the Republic of Iraq brought a claim against more than 90 defendants before the U.S. District Court of the Southern District of New York to recover damages stemming from alleged corruption in the context of the United Nations Oil-for-Food humanitarian aid program. That program, established in 1995, was designed to permit Iraq to sell oil to third parties in order to purchase humanitarian goods (food and medicine). The program was aimed at providing relief to Iraqi citizens from the international economic sanctions. The Republic of Iraq initiated a civil action to recover the surcharges on oil sales in its own right, to redress injury to its proprietary interests, and also "parens patriae, for the benefit of the Iraqi people," to redress injury to its quasi-sovereign interests.

Standing to recover for an injury to its proprietary interests was granted because the wrongful depletion of the UN escrow account could cause both particular and personal harm to Iraq, which had a concrete, if not exclusive, interest in the funds held in the UN escrow account. However, the court concluded that the Republic of Iraq did not have standing to recover as "parens patriae" for injuries to its people. Iraq specifically alleged that "defendants forced the Iraqi people to fund the payment of bribes designed to extend the reign of the tyrannical regime that subjected them" and that defendants "siphoned off" program funds and contributed to "shortages of food and medicine" that exacerbated the suffering of the Iraqi people. The court reminded that even though the U.S. Supreme Court has endorsed standing for states of the United States and Puerto Rico on parens patriae grounds, it has never recognized standing for foreign states solely on those grounds. Interesting from a standing point of view, the Republic of Iraq's claims were not successful.

Note: See Republic of Iraq v. ABB AG et al., Case: 08 Civ. 5951 (SHS), February 6, 2013.

Alamieyeseigha was governor of Bayelsa state from May 1999 until his impeachment in September 2005. In November 2005, Nigeria's Economic and Financial Crimes Commission charged him criminally with 40 counts of money laundering and corruption.[a] He pleaded guilty in Nigeria in 2007 to charges of falsely declaring his assets. His companies pleaded guilty to money laundering,[b] and the court seized his assets in Nigeria. More recently, in 2013, he was pardoned.[c]

As a result of civil lawsuits that Nigeria filed abroad, more than US$17 million worth of assets abroad were confiscated and repatriated to Nigeria as constituting the proceeds of crime. The process was challenging, particularly regarding the location of the bank accounts, because assets and evidence were located in many places, such as the Bahamas, the British Virgin Islands, South Africa, Cyprus, Denmark, the United States, and the United Kingdom.

Realizing that requesting mutual legal assistance in a criminal case would be time consuming and that orders from Nigerian courts would not necessarily be executed by all foreign jurisdictions, Nigeria brought civil proceedings in the United Kingdom. The application was allowed by the U.K. court. In rulings in 2006 and 2007, based on the U.K. Proceeds of Crime Act, the London High Court of Justice held that Nigeria was the true owner of three residential properties in London (registered under Solomon & Peters Ltd. as sole proprietor) and of the credit balances of certain bank accounts, amounting to approximately US$2.7 million (held at the Royal Bank of Scotland in the name of Santolina Investment Corporation), as well as US$1.5 million seized at the time of arrest. It turned out that Santolina was a corporate vehicle hiding assets related to the offshore jurisdictions. The total amount recovered exceeded US$17.7 million.

Note: See Nigeria v. Santolina Investment Corp. and Ors. [2007] EWHC 3053 (Q.B.) (UK High Court decision in Nigeria v. Santolina Investment Corp. and Ors. December 3, 2007 Case No: HC05 CO3602).
a. London High Court of Justice, Diepreye Solomon Peter Alamieyeseigha v. The Crown Prosecution Services, 25 November 2005, Case No: CO/9133/2005.
b. See Federal High Court of Nigeria, Lagos, Federal Republic of Nigeria v. Diepreye Alamieyeseigha & Ors., Suit No. FHC/U328C/05.
c. On March 13, 2013, the Senior Special Assistant for Public Affairs to President Goodluck Jonathan, Doyin Okupe, reported to Channels Television's breakfast program, "Sunrise Daily," that the Council of States granted a state pardon to the former Bayelsa state governor, Diepreye Alamieyeseigha, http://www.channelstv.com/home/2013/03/13/okupe-confirms-pardon-for-ex-convicts-alamieyeisegha-diya-others/.

a civil party in the criminal proceedings. To obtain civil party status, states and other government entities must show that they suffered loss or damage resulting directly from the offense. Then the claim for compensation of damages can be adjudicated within the criminal trial. This option is available in most civil law jurisdictions under the codes of criminal procedure.

In Switzerland, for example, Article 122, paragraph 1 of the Code of Criminal Procedure provides that "[t]he person suffering harm may bring civil claims based on the

This action was a claim by the federal republic of Brazil and the municipality of São Paulo to certain funds, US$10.5 million plus interest, held in bank accounts in Jersey in the name of the defendants, M. Maluf, former mayor of São Paulo and governor of São Paulo state, and his son Flavio, an active businessman in Brazil.

The plaintiffs, state and municipality, accused the Malufs of holding bank accounts in Jersey banks containing the traceable proceeds of bribes, secret commissions, or other fraudulent payments ("kickbacks") received by the defendant companies, Durant and Kildaire, in connection with major public works contracts in São Paulo. The individual defendants allegedly received the money through the two defendant companies, which they controlled or owned in practice. The state and the municipality asserted a proprietary claim, meaning that they were reasserting control over their own property.

The Royal Court of Jersey accepted both claims, stating that the federal republic of Brazil is "constitutionally a necessary party to any claim brought outside Brazil by a public authority" and that the municipality of São Paulo "is the substantively aggrieved party." In 2012, the Royal Court of Jersey found that the defendants were liable to the plaintiffs as a constructive trustee, on the basis of unjust enrichment, and ordered the defendants to pay a sum exceeding US$10 million plus interest.

Note: Republic of Brazil v. Durant, JRC [Isle of Jersey] 211 (2012). The decision was affirmed by the Court of Appeals on April 11, 2013, http://www.jerseylaw.je/judgments/unreportedjudgments/documents/display.aspx?url=2013%2F13-04-11_Republic _of_Brazil-v-Durant_JCA071.htm.

offense as a private claimant in the criminal proceedings." On this basis, foreign states seeking the return of corruptly acquired assets are often permitted to be a civil party to Swiss criminal investigations or proceedings concerning those assets (see box 1.6). If granted, that status will allow the foreign state access to documents including the court's criminal files, allow it to participate in the examination of witnesses and to make submissions to the investigating magistrate, and finally, permit it to seek the repatriation of the assets.[11]

Similarly in France, under Article 2 of the French Criminal Procedure Code, a party may obtain civil compensation from a criminal court when the party can show personal and direct damage resulting from the crime. Victims that have directly suffered from a crime may bring a claim before the competent investigative judge and seek to be

---

11. Arvinder Sambei, *Civil Forfeiture (confiscation in rem): Explanatory and Impact Study*, Council of Europe, technical paper, 2012, http://www.coe.int/t/dghl/cooperation/economiccrime/corruption/projects/car_serbia/Technical%20papers/2358%20CAR%20-%20TP%2020%20-%20Arvinder%20Sambei%20-%20Impact%20Study%20on%20Civil%20Forfeiture%20-%20May%202012%20-%20ENG%20(2).pdf.

BOX 1.5	A State-Owned Entity Obtains Bribe Money Held in a Foreign Bank Account through a Civil Claim in a Foreign Court: *Kartika Ratna Thahir v. Pertamina* (Singapore)

Pertamina is an Indonesian state-owned company created in 1971. Pertamina undertook major economic development projects at the direction of the Indonesian government. Foreign contractors paid bribes to Haji Achmad Thahir, an executive at Pertamina, to obtain more favorable contractual terms and preferential treatment. Pertamina sued to recover the bribes.

The bribes had been deposited by M. Thahir into bank accounts located in a Singaporean bank. Pertamina learned about these bank accounts (held jointly by M. Thahir and his wife, Mrs. Kartika Ratna Thahir) after the death of M. Thahir. Pertamina brought an action in Singapore claiming those funds. The courts of first instance and appeal accepted the claim of Pertamina, emphasizing that "having regard to the far reaching extent of [M. Thahir's] duties and responsibilities (…) it is difficult to envisage any clearer situation giving rise to a fiduciary relationship," and therefore the assets were returned to the state-owned company.

Note: Thahir Kartika Ratna v. PT Pertambangan Minyakdan Gas Bumi Negara (Pertamina) [1994] 3 SLR (R) 312; [1994] SGCA 105, http://www.singaporelaw.sg/sglaw/laws-of-singapore/case-law/cases-in-articles/equity-and-trusts/1494-thahir-kartika-ratna-v -pt-pertambangan-minyak-dan-gas-bumi-negara-pertamina-1994-3-slr-r-312-1994-sgca-105KartikaRatnaThahir v. PT Pertambangan Minyakdan Gas Bumi Negara (Pertamina), [1994] 3 SLR 257; [1994] SGCA 105.

BOX 1.6	State as Civil Party: Tunisia Granted Status as *Partie Civile* in Switzerland and Other Countries in Criminal Cases Involving Stolen Assets

After the fall of former Tunisian president Ben Ali, criminal proceedings were opened in, among other places, France, Switzerland, and Italy, to implement a European regulation ordering the freezing of all assets belonging to him and his family.

Tunisia hired lawyers in the main jurisdictions concerned to intervene as *"partie civile"* in the criminal case. That allowed a direct discussion with the investigative judge and close monitoring of the criminal proceedings.

Note: An important Swiss decision may be found at BB.2011.130 TPF (March 20, 2012, Federal Criminal Court).

recognized as *"partie civile."*[12] If granted, this status as *"partie civile"* permits a state to be a full party to the criminal proceedings. A state may also request action by judicial authorities and may closely monitor any actions taken by the investigative judge.[13]

---

12. Article 85, *Code de Procédure Pénale* [France].
13. See, for example, box 4.13, in chapter 4, concerning the case of Nigeria v. Santolina Investment Corp. and Ors., in which Nigeria was awarded damages as *partie civile* to a criminal money laundering case against a Nigerian official in France; *Tribunal de Grand Instance (TGI) de Paris, 11ᵉᵐᵉ chambre*, November 7, 2007.

Similar procedures exist in the postsocialist states of Central and Eastern Europe, particularly the successor states to the former Yugoslavia. In those jurisdictions, they are commonly referred to as claims under property law in criminal proceedings.[14] In Bosnia, for instance, Articles 193 to 204 of chapter 17 of the Bosnian Criminal Procedure Code provide for claims under property law relevant to reimbursement of damage, recovery of items, or annulment of a particular legal transaction (box 1.7).[15] Additional discussion of the civil party to a criminal case is provided in chapter 4.

B. Defendants: Who Can Be Sued?

A defendant in a civil lawsuit is the person or entity against whom relief or recovery is being sought by the plaintiff. In bribery cases, jurisdictions have often considered the potential defendants through the lens of the principal/agent relationship. As such, in any civil case related to damages caused by corrupt acts, the obvious defendant is the corrupt agent or the briber. However, grand corruption schemes are generally complex, and in a wider perspective, defendants might include intermediaries as well.

1. The Agency Relationship in Civil Cases Involving Bribery

Conceptually, the core of corruption is sometimes defined as an agency problem: The "agent," whether an elected politician, appointed official, or employee, has a duty

---

14. See, for example, chapter 17 of the Bosnian Criminal Procedure Code, Articles 193 to 204.

15. Criminal Procedure Code of Bosnia and Herzegovina, unofficial, consolidated version, partially reviewed by the Registry Language Unit of the Prosecutor's Office of Bosnia and Herzegovina, 2009, http://www.icrc .org/applic/ihl/ihl-nat.nsf/0/904fb6c00dbd0b8ac12576d5004cda83/$FILE/Criminal_Procedure_Code _of_BH_-_consolidated_version_dec2009.pdf.

FIGURE 1.2   Who Can the Principal Sue in Bribery Cases?

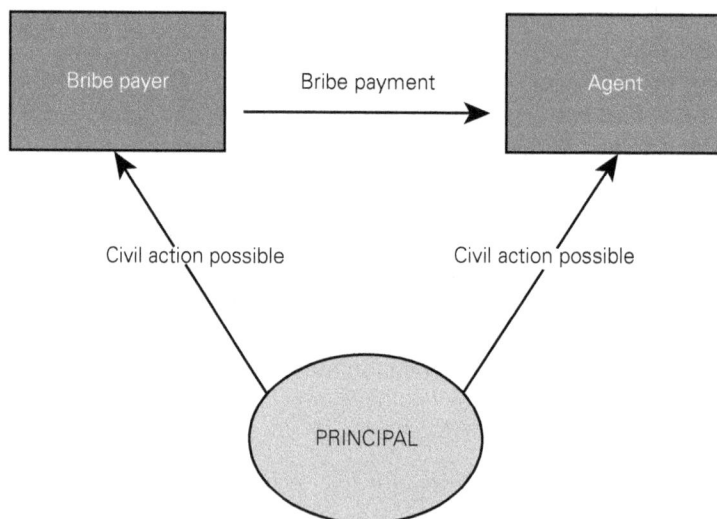

Source: World Bank.

to act in the interests of someone else, called the "principal." Therefore, the concept of the principal-agent relationship may prove valuable to identify the defendants who can be sued in bribery cases. A typical corruption case in this regard would involve three persons: the employer-principal, the employee-agent, and the client-bribe payer.

An agency relationship may be characterized as a contract under which two persons (or entities) are linked by a special relationship: when the agent agrees to act for the benefit of the principal, and not in his personal interest, he has a legal duty called a "fiduciary duty." A fiduciary duty is defined as a legal duty to act solely in another party's interests. If the agent receives a bribe from someone, he breaches his fiduciary duty. The principal can then seek recovery for the breach of duty committed by the agent for that agent's own interest. Figure 1.2 and box 1.8 illustrate this concept.

The principal-agent model covers most cases of bribery that arise in practice. However, the scope of this book goes beyond bribery cases, and the triangular relationship may not be relevant for other civil wrongs.

2. The Array of Potential Defendants in Civil Lawsuits

As previously observed, in civil suits seeking to recover damages caused by corrupt activities, the obvious defendant would be the corrupt official or the briber payer. An element to consider when seeking to recover the proceeds of corruption from corrupt officials is potential political immunities from criminal prosecution, or even from civil suits, that they might enjoy.

An Example of the Principal/Agent Relationship: *Continental Management v. United States* (United States)

In the case *Continental Management v. United States*, the United States government, as the principal, sued a public official who misused his position for private gain. The court held that the agent/public official/employee's receipt of secret profits injured the principal/employer "because it necessarily creates a conflict of interest and tends to subvert the agent's loyalty."[a]

The principal who has suffered harm as a result of his agent's corrupt activity can typically seek damages and restitution. To obtain civil remedies, there must typically be some sort of fiduciary relationship between the parties to the litigation. In general, both the employee/agent and the bribe payer are liable to the principal/employer for damages and restitution.

Source: Keith Henderson and Karen Aguida, "United States," in *Private Commercial Bribery,* edited by Günter Heine, Barbara Huber, and Thomas O. Rose, 479, 548 (Friburg and Paris: Iuscrim and International Chamber of Commerce, 2003).

a. Continental Management Inc. v. United States, 208 Ct. Cl. 501, 527 F.2d. 613, 617 (1975).

However, very few corrupt officials hold assets in their own names. Thus relatives, close associates, or corporate vehicles controlled by the corrupt official are possible defendants as well. In addition to those claims, a plaintiff may sue third parties or intermediaries, such as banks, accountants, lawyers, art dealers, real estate agents, or others who worked with the wrongdoers. In particular, a victim may be able to claim damages against those assisting in a breach of fiduciary duty. For instance, if a financial institution holds stolen assets, it may be in breach of a general duty of care in the performance of financial services, and that may give rise to a claim.[16] The participation of the financial institution might be critical, for instance, in helping the corrupt official to steal, conceal, and perhaps launder the proceeds of the corrupt acts.

A plaintiff can sue persons who knowingly assisted in the concealment of assets or who received those assets as intermediaries in the laundering of proceeds of corruption. To prevail, the plaintiff will likely need to show that the intermediary knowingly assisted in the furtherance of the fraudulent activities or a dishonest breach of fiduciary duty. As noted earlier, if the intermediary can be proved to have acted knowingly along with the corrupt official, the intermediary may be liable for the full amount of the harm. Civil liability could be sought on this ground and would depend mostly on how the court interpreted the particular facts of the case, as the line between negligence or incompetence and willingly turning a "blind eye" can be very blurred and subjective (box 1.9).

Actions against these professionals may be difficult to prove. Often the plaintiff has to show actual knowledge on the part of the third party involved in a conspiracy or

---

16. Colin Nicholls QC, Timothy Daniel, Alan Bacarese, and John Hatchard, *Corruption and Misuse of Public Office,* 2d ed. (New York: Oxford University Press, 2011), 306.

Liability of Law Firms Used to Allegedly Conceal Monies: *Attorney General of Zambia v. Meer Care & Desai (a firm) & Ors.* (United Kingdom)

Frederick Chiluba was president of Zambia from 1991 until 2002. After he left office, the Zambian authorities began a criminal investigation and also convened a task force on asset recovery. In 2004, the attorney general of Zambia filed a civil lawsuit in the United Kingdom on behalf of the people of Zambia. The claim was that Chiluba, together with former Zambian officials, had conspired with others fraudulently to misappropriate monies that belonged to Zambia. Zambia alleged the money was the proceeds of corrupt schemes and that two English solicitors and their respective law firms, Iqbal Meer, of Meer Care & Desai, and Bimal Tacker, of Cave Malik, gave dishonest assistance in the misappropriation. The firms' bank accounts in London had allegedly been used in the payment of about US$20 million by the Zambian government pursuant to an alleged arms deal.

The judge at first instance had to decide "whether or not [Iqbal Meer] has crossed the line between being incompetent to being dishonest ("fool or knave")"[a] and if he was then liable for "dishonest assistance in a breach of fiduciary duty."[b] The judge found that the lawyer dishonestly assisted Chiluba and the Zambian defendants in their misconduct and had conspired to misappropriate monies from Zambia. The judge relied on the "constructive trust for dishonest assistance" theory. He considered that the partner either knew that the instructions he had carried out involved, in effect, handling stolen money, or he had had a clear suspicion that that was the case, which he chose to ignore (literally the "blind eye" definition).

On appeal, the higher court reversed and decided that the two codefendant lawyers were not liable.[c] The behavior of Iqbal Meer was again analyzed against the "fool or knave" test. The appellate judge stated that if "the [first instance] judge was clearly right to say that the course that Mr. Meer set out upon required caution, of which Mr. Meer seemed to be wholly unaware, and that Mr. Meer did not apply proper professional standards of caution in relation to the process, that is not sufficient to establish liability, and of itself might point away from dishonesty and towards incompetence. Mr. Meer's evidence about [...] issues relevant to money-laundering itself suggests to us that he was inexperienced in the relevant area, and naïve or foolish or both."[d] Thus the partner found liable for dishonest assistance was decided to be honest, albeit foolish, sometimes very foolish, and far from competent in his understanding, application, and observance of relevant professional duties, above all the need to comply with warnings about money laundering. Therefore, the appeal court "[allowed] Mr Meer's appeal against the judge's finding that he was liable to Zambia in conspiracy and on the basis of dishonest assistance" and "set aside the judge's orders against Mr Meer [...] and the firm, in both [its] orders dated 4 May 2007 and 29 June 2007, and [...] [dismissed] the claim against Mr. Meer [...] and the firm." Consequently, the first instance's order condemning Mr. Meer and the law firm to pay to Zambia more than US$11 million was dismissed.

(continued next page)

(continued)

This case demonstrates the difficulty of proving the liability of professionals (lawyers, bankers, accountants) who are involved in the management of stolen assets. This is perhaps an unusual example in that the professional adviser avoided liability due to his own incompetence. Such a defense may not be valid in most cases. In any event, victims should consider such action to claim damages against third parties, as the underlying legal theory of the "blind eye" was accepted, even if the proof was found lacking in that particular case.

Notes:
a. Attorney General of Zambia v. Meer Care & Desai (a firm) & Ors.[2007], EWHC 952 (Ch), para. 556.
b. Ibid., para. 332.
c. Attorney General of Zambia v. Meer Care & Desai (a firm) & Ors.[2008], EWCA Civ 1007.
d. Ibid., para. 280.

TABLE 1.1	Types of Defendants and Case Law Examples
Type of defendant	**Case law examples**
Corrupt public officials (the "Agents")	Hong Kong v. Reid (box 4.3); City of Cannes (box 7.2)
Companies and other legal entities controlling or holding assets for a corrupt official	Libya v. Capitana (box 4.1), Nigeria v. Santolina (boxes 1.3, 4.2, 4.13, and 5.5)
Family and cronies of the corrupt official who assist and hold assets	The Chiluba cases (boxes 1.9, 3.2, 4.11, and 8.1); the Dariye cases (boxes 3.1 and 8.3)
Officers of government entities	Pertamina (boxes 1.5 and 4.4)
Bribe payers	Alba v. Alcoa (box 3.4)
Third parties/intermediaries, such as trustees, bankers, accountants, lawyers	The Chiluba cases (boxes 1.9, 3.2, 4.11, and 8.1)
Source: World Bank.	

present facts from which a reasonable person should have known of the dishonest behavior. Nonetheless, it may sometimes be worthwhile to file a claim. One possible collateral benefit is that new information collected in the course of the lawsuit may provide the basis for more promising claims. In addition, because entities such as banks may have branches in many locations and may possess considerable assets, such an action may be an easier and more fruitful starting point than going after the corrupt official directly.

Finally, table 1.1 summarizes the major types of defendants against which states and other government entities may consider pursuing a civil lawsuit arising from corrupt acts.

2. Hiring an Attorney: Steps, Considerations, and Fee Arrangements

If a state decides that all or part of the proceeds of certain corruption offenses is to be recovered using civil law methods, it will need to identify attorneys to consult to begin to formulate claims and develop an international asset recovery strategy. Hiring attorneys for particular civil asset recovery proceedings may be challenging, but with careful preparation, government actors will be able to identify a qualified attorney; structure a fee arrangement that suits the needs of the particular case; if necessary, consider funding the lawsuit with a commercial litigation fund; and request potential assistance from international organizations.

A. Identifying a Suitable Attorney

1. Qualities of an Effective Asset-Recovery Attorney

Asset recovery actions provide unique challenges: The money is almost never hidden in the country from which it is stolen; the money is rarely hidden in just one jurisdiction. Usually a multiplicity of persons or institutions is involved in the transfer of assets. The money must be traced, and the bank or other institution where the money is on deposit must be contacted. An effective asset recovery attorney must be familiar with these challenges and with effective responses to them.

Asset recovery cases are often politically sensitive, as well, both in the country from which the money was stolen and in the countries where it has been hidden. The attorney should be politically savvy and able to navigate multiple political systems in a diplomatic, yet effective, way. Within a country, there may not be agreement on the asset recovery process itself because of political opposition; allies of the corrupt official may remain in power or retain influence. The attorney must be able to communicate with, and sometimes coordinate communication among, government actors in each country, as well as other various domestic stakeholders.

Furthermore, many corrupt officials have become very wealthy and hence are able to hire the best lawyers and accountants to help them protect the assets or delay their return while the assets are spent or hidden further. They will form multijurisdictional teams and joint defense agreements. Frequently assets may be hidden in the names of family members or associates, who will also contest the recovery, leading to additional expense and delays in the recovery of the assets. In such an environment, the government's asset recovery attorney must have sufficient knowledge of the field to counter sophisticated legal maneuvering on the part of the defendants.

The attorney should be generally familiar with the legal systems of implicated countries and willing and able to work with counsel in other countries (see box 2.1). Though this book deals only with civil remedies, if the government is considering bringing a concurrent or later criminal action the attorney must be aware of the consequences of her or his efforts on potential criminal liability. Some jurisdictions have very strict rules governing disclosure, and the attorney must be careful not to prejudice the possibility of criminal liability while pursuing civil remedies.

State plaintiffs must bear in mind that the multijurisdictional nature of asset recovery litigation will usually require them to hire counsels in different jurisdictions and to ensure that they can work as a team. Most often, one attorney (or even a single law firm) will be insufficient to pursue a complex, multijurisdictional asset recovery matter. Moreover, the attorneys may need to identify and hire additional experts, including specialists such as forensic accountants, investigators, and other attorneys. Identifying a suitable attorney also involves some preliminary thought about where to sue (discussed in the next chapter), as one generally needs an attorney licensed and practiced in the jurisdiction where the suit is brought. One approach to address these concerns

---

BOX 2.1   Qualities of a Successful Asset Recovery Attorney

- Preferably, prior experience with asset recovery cases in relevant jurisdictions
- Politically connected and experienced
- Reputation for integrity in courts and governments
- Familiarity with relevant national law regimes
- Some knowledge of comparative law and understanding of different legal systems in common and civil law jurisdictions
- Awareness of potential consequences of the civil action on any criminal suit contemplated by the government
- Ability to work with counsel in other countries
- Ability to lead a team of experts (forensic accountants, investigators, etc.)
- Access to experienced experts
- Reasonably priced
- Insurance for professional negligence, covering the amount sought and including legal advice on foreign law (you usually need a special insurance policy for this)

Source: World Bank.

about the international dimension of asset recovery cases is to hire a single, multinational law firm, with a worldwide reach. Such firms do have expertise across jurisdictions and can easily hire local counsel if need be. Another approach is to hire directly counsel in the jurisdictions of interest.

2. State Legal Representation

Often priority goes to private attorneys located in the jurisdiction where the claim will likely be brought, as knowledge of local laws and procedures may be decisive in the case. In a few states the government employs attorneys who are empowered to handle civil matters on the part of the state, and who possibly could assist foreign states. These attorneys may be able to evaluate where to file a case and even to present it before a local court. In the few jurisdictions where that is possible, hiring a lawyer may not be necessary. For example, in Brazil, public attorneys are dedicated to the state's legal representation before local courts, not only in criminal matters but civil matters as well. In Italy, the *Avvocato Generale dello Stato* is in charge of representing the state in any civil, criminal, or administrative lawsuit but is not in charge of prosecution.

This kind of structure may extend to benefits in the area of international cooperation. Brazil and Italy, for instance, adopted a memorandum of understanding (MoU) on cooperation in state legal representation.[1] According to the MoU, each party shall appear before its local courts to represent the interests of the other party, provided that the latter has so requested and the interests of both states are not incompatible.[2] Based on the agreement, Brazil could have the support of being represented by Italian state attorneys before Italian courts in asset recovery cases. In addition, in some countries, such as South Africa, state attorneys are authorized by law to promote, subject to certain conditions, the legal representation of foreign States.[3] Albeit still rare, these modalities of cooperation between states could avoid costs entailed in contracts with private lawyers.

3. Public Procurement Rules

In the process of identifying and selecting a suitable attorney, states often confront strict rules governing public procurement that constrain use of public funds to hire private attorneys. These rules differ from one jurisdiction to another. The main difficulty is that government procurement rules often lead to hiring the service provider that offers the cheapest price at a minimum quality standard. Some specialized services, however,

---

1. Memorandum of Understanding between the Office of the Attorney General of the Union (Brazil) and the Office of the Attorney General of the State (Italy), of April 11, 2014.
2. Ibid., Article 2 (a).
3. Republic of South Africa, State Attorney Amendment Bill (2013), section 9A: "Performance by offices of State Attorney of work on behalf of government of foreign state. If agreed upon between the Government of the Republic and the government of any other state, an office of State Attorney may perform such kind of work as is performed under this Act by the said office on behalf of the Government of the Republic, for or on behalf of the government of that other state in any court or in any part of the Republic or in that state, subject to such conditions as may be so agreed upon."

such as legal advice and representation, may not be fully compatible with the process of public procurement. It is paramount that the qualities expected in an attorney and mentioned above should guide states in the selection process, even if exemptions or exceptions to procurement rules need to be sought. Some countries—Brazil, for example—have adopted special regimes for the process of selecting private attorneys to represent the state before foreign courts.[4] Generally, legal fees and costs play an important role, but they should not be decisive in the selection of a legal counsel. In some cases the adage, "You get what you pay for," is true in the realm of legal services.

Moreover, if typical public procurement procedures are followed (announcements, bids, etc.), it would provide the defendants with advance notice of the government's civil recovery strategy. Thus, those procedures should be replaced, when legally allowed, with short-list procurement, which is also quicker. As most large recovery cases are by essence multijurisdictional, it may make sense to contract a lead law firm that may, on instructions of the client, subcontract additional law firms in other jurisdictions. Otherwise, hiring a new law firm through public procurement, or even short-listing, will entail delays that are incompatible with a successful asset recovery strategy.

For example, if the victimized state, through participation as *partie civile* in Swiss criminal proceedings, learns of the existence of a bank account in Hong Kong SAR, China, where freezing orders through mutual assistance are notoriously difficult to obtain, its only option would be to hire a local law firm to request a civil freezing order, which may need to be obtained urgently and under local law can be had in less than 24 hours. If the hiring of a Hong Kong SAR, China, firm requires weeks or months, the Hong Kong SAR, China, bank account will in all likelihood have been emptied. However, if the lead law firm hires a local law firm, the freezing order can be obtained. It should also be noted that whereas large international law firms have strong asset recovery capacity and experience in the United Kingdom and the United States, their offices in less-central jurisdictions are likely to lack specialization in asset recovery; they will have to hire local firms and will face the same problem. There are no easy answers to procurement issues, but proceeding carefully, and treating the hiring of asset recovery attorneys as out of the norm, will be of assistance.

4. Search for an Attorney and Due Diligence

Although the need for confidence and speed may necessitate hiring an attorney quickly, regardless of whether the hiring process is public or private, the government should use due diligence to ensure that the one hired is the best attorney for the job. Governments may follow up with counterparts in other countries to find out which attorneys were used in other cases and to what effect. This due diligence should, at a minimum, involve following up on references.

Another way to verify the competence of potential attorneys is through a detailed online search focusing on unbiased sources. In addition to newspaper articles, governments

---

4. See Law n. 8.897 of 1994, article 4, *Casa Civil, Subchefia para Assuntos Jurídicos,* http://www.planalto.gov .br/ccivil_03/Leis/1989_1994/L8897.htm and Decree n. 7.598 of 2011.

should become familiar with the various organizations, rating agencies, and bar associations that track asset recovery attorneys and individual case outcomes. For example, World Bank and UN publications,[5] the International Chamber of Commerce (ICC) Corruption Unit,[6] and U4[7] may mention particular outcomes, and through research one can determine who the successful attorneys were. Ratings agencies increasingly include asset recovery listings; organizations such as FraudNet, the International Chamber of Commerce, the World Bank's Corruption Hunters Alliance list, and Chambers and Partners (an online attorney ranking service), for example, rank active asset recovery attorneys. An individual lawyer might also be a member of the Anti-Corruption Committees of the International Bar Association or the American Bar Association. Researching past conferences on asset recovery also may identify lawyers who have written extensively on corruption and asset recovery issues or spoken on them at such conferences. No single one of these sources is dispositive, but together they may create a cumulative picture of an attorney's experience and successes in asset recovery.

After identifying several potential attorneys, the government may invite the attorneys to present their qualifications and proposed terms of engagement in interviews or presentations. Colloquially, among lawyers, this is known as a "beauty parade." The government may describe the proposed civil litigation and ask the attorney her or his thoughts on whether and how the case should best proceed. Under canons of legal ethics in almost all countries, the attorney would be bound to keep secret what is discussed even at this stage. Interviewing several attorneys will give the government a better understanding of the different asset recovery approaches available and the range of fees and expenses that may be charged. The government can use the information to better negotiate the terms of the engagement.

The government should ensure that the attorney is free from conflicts of interest. For example, if the law firm of a potential attorney represents a bank or another defendant that appears to be an intermediary that could become a defendant in the litigation, that would pose a problem. Moreover, some attorneys may seek an exclusive right to represent the client government in asset recovery cases, and even to control all hiring of third parties. Governments should beware of such a request, as it is rarely in the client's interest and may lead to grossly inflated expenses and even legal entanglements. Such a "monopoly" is contrary to the team approach that is usually best suited to international asset recovery in the long term.

During the interview stage, the government actor and the attorney should together identify the best possible outcome for the litigation and agree on potential steps toward that outcome. Sometimes law firms are willing to include free services outside the scope of the asset recovery litigation, such as training for government attorneys. If extra

---

5. The Stolen Asset Recovery Initiative (StAR), http://star.worldbank.org/star/.
6. International Chamber of Commerce, http://www.iccwbo.org/advocacy-codes-and-rules/areas-of-work/corporate-responsibility-and-anti-corruption/.
7. U4, The Anti-Corruption Resource Centre, http://www.u4.no/.

services are offered, they should be identified at this initial stage and confirmed in writing in the engagement letter.

The government should also understand any public disclosure requirements that may apply to the lawyer (for example, in the United States, they may be required to register with the U.S. government as an agent of the foreign government, with a statutory requirement to disclose the terms of the engagement and any assets recovered), as well as any intentions of the attorney regarding publicity of the engagement. For example, does the attorney intend to publicize the engagement on their website, to include it in marketing materials to other clients, or to announce it in attorney trade publications? Eventually some aspects, such as fees arrangements with attorneys, may become a matter of public record in court orders or settlements. Nonetheless, most terms are negotiable, and the state as client should strive for what it wants at the best price-to-quality ratio (box 2.2). The charts in figures 2.1 and 2.2 illustrate the positive and negative factors that are decisive when selecting an attorney.

When an attorney is chosen, the agreement between the attorney and the government actor should be as clear as possible regarding fee arrangements, reporting requirements, and the extent of control the government expects to have over each stage of the litigation.

BOX 2.2 Identifying a Suitable Attorney

- References from other governments or agencies that have brought civil claims
  - Prior success in asset recovery litigation
  - Recommendation from other litigating country
- Online research
  - Newspapers
  - International organizations
  - Ratings agencies
  - Membership in asset recovery or anticorruption groups
  - Speeches and publications by the potential attorney on asset recovery
- Interviews
  - The potential attorney's general sense of the case
  - Experience
  - Freedom from potential conflicts of interest
  - Satisfactory fee arrangements
  - Requirements regarding confidentiality, publicity, and public disclosure

Source: World Bank.

FIGURE 2.1   Selecting an Attorney—The Caution Flags

No reputation
as excellent
lawyer

No past case

Not member of
prestigious
professional group

No international work

Not licensed
where assets
are

No
countries
as clients

No experience
enforcing foreign
judgments

No experience in
freezing/seizing
assets

No experience with
experts, accountants,
or investigators

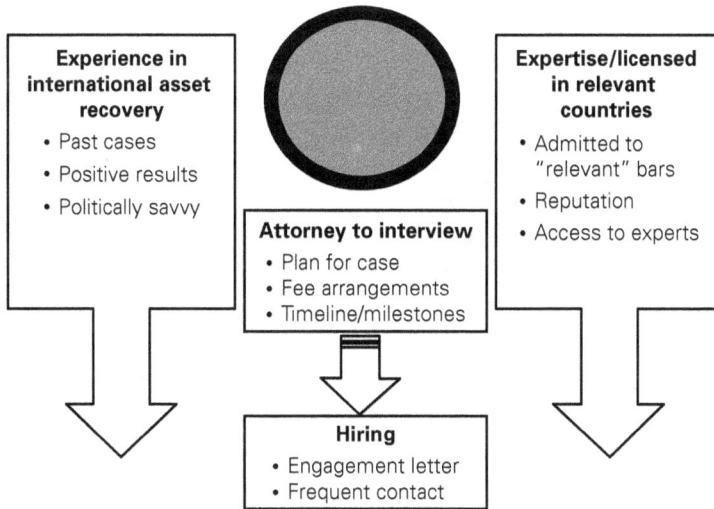

Source: World Bank.

FIGURE 2.2   Selecting an Attorney—The Green Lights

**Experience in
international asset
recovery**
- Past cases
- Positive results
- Politically savvy

**Expertise/licensed
in relevant
countries**
- Admitted to
  "relevant" bars
- Reputation
- Access to experts

Attorney to interview
- Plan for case
- Fee arrangements
- Timeline/milestones

Hiring
- Engagement letter
- Frequent contact

Source: World Bank.

B. Structuring a Fee Arrangement

In the structuring of fee arrangements, needs may vary depending on the jurisdiction. For example, some jurisdictions do not permit so-called contingency fees, which are fees based on a percentage of the assets recovered. Therefore several elements should be considered before a government enters into a fee arrangement. Various types of fee arrangements are at the disposal of states and government entities.

1. Considerations in Structuring a Fee Arrangement

Before any attorney is hired, the government and the potential attorney should work together to estimate the costs of a particular case. That may be difficult: It may not be clear where the assets have gone or how they may be hidden. The government may not know the extent of the stolen assets or how much the corrupt actors or their relatives and associates—the opposing side—are willing and able to spend to keep them. Initial agreements may be contingent on what is found in the first few weeks of inquiry. However, an experienced attorney should be able to give an estimated range of costs.

Once an attorney has been identified, the parties should negotiate a satisfactory fee arrangement in writing. Structuring a fee arrangement may be politically sensitive. Government actors should consider constituent expectations; residents of a country may be justly angry that their country's money has been stolen. It may be politically sensitive to announce that money has been recovered but a large percentage of the recovery will go to lawyers rather than the people of the country. Governments should assume that, despite their best efforts at confidentiality, information about the fee arrangements may become public. The lawyer may be concerned that possible regime change or other political events may harm his ability to collect on promised fees.

Though civil asset recovery has many motivations, including making certain that no one benefits from his own wrongdoing, governments should have in mind that a risk exists of spending more money to recover the assets than the assets are worth. A fee structure should take that into account, allowing a case to be dropped if it seems likely to become so expensive that it would be impractical to pursue. As the litigation progresses, the government should continually weigh the costs of litigation (incurred and anticipated future fees) versus likely outcomes. Some corrupt officials intentionally draw out asset recovery cases, causing them to become very costly.

For this reason, fee arrangements might include "staged" funding, in which payment for the next stage of the litigation is contingent on the government actor's agreeing to pursue the matter to the next step. For example, an initial fee agreement may include only the first two weeks of evaluating the strengths and weaknesses of the case. After the initial evaluation phase, the government may then agree to pursue the case to the next stage, and so on. At each stage, the government actor should require reporting against the agreed budget. Additionally a procedure should be agreed upon for discussing early signs that the budget may be exceeded. This oversight will also improve the transparency of the fees incurred and mitigate risks of excessive billing by the attorneys.

Considerations in structuring a fee arrangement may also include possible widening of the scope of engagement beyond a single case. Potentially the attorney selected may be hired not only to handle a particular case but also to provide legal counseling about strategies for asset recovery in general, in one or many jurisdictions, even before a decision to file a particular case elsewhere. This type of engagement may also be valuable for dealing with very urgent measures, as under some circumstances the state will not have time to go through all the steps necessary to obtain a contract if it is to initiate a timely legal action.

Within the government, clear agreement should be established on who will be the decision maker with regard to the litigation and whether there are to be any requirements for consultation or reporting on the progress. At certain stages, progress or lack thereof in the case may become a matter of public record. The government may wish to identify a media strategy, with a designated spokesperson who will be briefed in advance on developments in the case and will be tasked with responding to all media inquiries.

In addition to regular reporting, the attorney should communicate on an informal, frequent, and regular basis with the designated contact in the government. The minister of finance or justice will rarely be able to take on this role personally but should appoint a person with sufficient access and technical qualifications within the ministry to act as liaison between the government and the asset recovery attorney. The government contact person should be knowledgeable about any developments with regard either to the political situation or to other cases that could affect case outcomes. Results in asset recovery cases are generally better when the client government actively participates in the process and communicates regularly with the attorney. A dedicated liaison ensures that the attorney and the government consistently agree on the goals and means of the litigation (box 2.3).

BOX 2.3   Considerations in Structuring a Fee Arrangement

- Constituent and public expectations and the political context
- Initial estimate of fees and costs
- Ratio of expected recovery to expenditures
- Progress reporting:
  - Identification of intervals or stages at which reporting is required
  - Identification of dedicated government point person
  - Reevaluation of estimate of fees and costs at regular intervals
- Wider scope of engagement with the state

Source: World Bank.

2. Types of Fee Arrangements

There are several main varieties of fee arrangements and infinite variations:

Hourly. "Hourly rates" means the rate per hour for the attorney, multiplied by the number of hours worked. It is the most common fee arrangement in litigation. Some law firms offer a "blended" hourly rate, derived from the hourly rates charged by the various attorneys likely to be working on the matter. The most experienced attorneys cost more. However, they provide crucial judgment and expertise and may accomplish tasks in less time. Moreover, they may delegate legal research to more junior, less-expensive attorneys. Some law firms may agree to charge on an hourly basis, subject to an overall limit or cap on fees charged, unless there is a material change to the terms of the engagement.

Flat fee. A fixed or flat fee means that the attorney and government decide exactly how much the attorney will be paid for the case, or for a stage of the case, no matter the investment of time or resources. Although attractive because of the perceived certainty of the fee, flat fee arrangements are often difficult in practice. Attorneys may underinvest in the research necessary for success or may seek to renegotiate the fee at times when the government is vulnerable because of changed circumstances.

Contingency fee. In contingency fee arrangements, the lawyer is not paid until, and unless, assets are recovered. After recovery, the lawyer receives a certain, previously agreed percentage of the recovered monies. A note of caution: First, these arrangements are not permitted in many jurisdictions. Second, governments interested in entering into such arrangements should carefully consider how to define what will trigger the "success fee," so that they can avoid paying it in cases where recovery does not result from the lawyer's activity, or if the trigger occurs in the future many years after the lawyer has no longer been involved. For example, outcomes of this kind can occur in asset recovery cases that involve parallel criminal and civil actions. Finally, because the lawyer collects the fee in one visible lump sum, governments may suffer adverse publicity concerning a large proportion of the recovery going to lawyers.

"Hybrid" arrangements. This category includes any combination of the fee structures described above; such combinations are commonly used in asset recovery litigation. For example, perhaps the attorneys will agree to a reduced hourly rate in exchange for an increase in the standard rate once assets are recovered (see box 2.4).

Managing Expenses in the Fee Arrangement

The cost of actual legal services is not the only item for which attorneys bill a client. Many other costs and expenses—ranging from photocopying, to attorney travel, to hourly rates for law firm support personnel such as paralegals, to various other items—may be subject to negotiation or at the least should be clarified at the start of the engagement. Because such expenses can add up quickly, it is best at the outset to

- Flat fee

- Hourly rate (may be a blended hourly rate and may be subject to a cap)

- Contingency fee

- "Hybrid" (for example, a reduced hourly rate plus a small percentage of the assets recovered)

Source: World Bank.

determine what other costs and expenses the attorney anticipates and at what rate they will be billed. In other words, it is important to have an overview of all the costs associated with the litigation, not just legal fees.

The fee arrangement may be structured so that expenses will be limited to a specified amount on a monthly basis, or it may require authorization before expenses above a prescribed amount may be incurred (for example, expenses in excess of US$10,000 may be incurred only with the prior written authorization of the government). Parties may wish to agree on a policy statement on travel costs (for example, setting a limit on, or specifying the class of, travel, hotels, and the like, and per diem, if any). Reimbursement of reasonable out-of-pocket expenses will be made only with a sufficiently detailed invoice and documentation of the expenses. The government should ensure that all expenses, with supporting receipts as necessary, are included with sufficient detail in the attorney's invoices, so that the government can monitor compliance with the fee arrangements.

As the case may involve multiple jurisdictions or other complexities, it may also be necessary for attorneys from time to time to hire third parties such as forensic accountants, private investigators, or attorneys licensed to practice in other jurisdictions. The fee arrangement should include provisions for such engagements. For example, it may specify that third parties may not be engaged without the prior consent of the government if the fees and expenses of the third parties will exceed a specified amount. The government should be consulted to determine whether it already has existing relationships with other attorneys, forensic accountants, or investigators who may be able to perform the desired services. If not, the fee arrangement may specify that a competitive selection process be used and that any third party proposed by the attorney be required to disclose any potential conflicts of interest. The government may wish to require that its consent be obtained regarding the scope of the work to be performed by the third parties and the terms of their engagement (including applicable fees and expenses), as well as provision of detailed invoices for payments to third parties above a specified amount.

C. Litigation and Asset Recovery Funds

In some cases when the state has a meritorious claim, the cost of private litigation (including lawyers, investigators, experts, accountants, and others) is a serious impediment to its pursuit of civil proceedings. Moreover, states are accountable for, and would have to justify the use of, potentially scarce public funds to finance civil proceedings to recover stolen assets. This can be challenging for states even in situations where the estimated costs of litigation amount to a slight percentage of the assets being claimed. In that context, "litigation funding," a relatively new phenomenon in asset recovery and other fields, may appear as an attractive option.

Litigation funding is a mechanism by which litigants can finance their litigation and other legal costs through a third party funding company. These "litigation funds" are mainly for-profit commercial organizations (mostly banks, hedge funds, and private investors) that fund in whole or in part the legal costs of a party to litigation or arbitration, in exchange for a percentage of the recovery. Some nonprofit entities may also operate such funds. Litigation funds finance only the lawsuits that they think are likely to succeed. They look at indicators such as the claim value, the estimated costs, the merits of the claim, the recoverability, and the experience of the legal team running the claim. Funders may also analyze jurisdictions in which the assets are likely to be found and judge what barriers to recovery are likely to arise (that is, the provisions of national law on enforcement, political risks, or any beneficial ownership issues).[8] These relationships are diagrammed in figure 2.3.

For better or worse, however, governments should be aware of the extent to which the litigation fund, not the government, may direct the course of certain aspects of the litigation and the asset recovery scheme. Employees of litigation funds tend to be involved with the lawsuits they finance; they perform due diligence on attorneys and ensure appropriate experience. They often release the funding in stages, holding funds for a later stage until it is apparent that earlier stages were worthwhile and calculating the risk versus the probability of success.

Government actors must recognize that if the litigation fund manager ceases to believe that successful recovery is likely, funding may cease. A contrary view by the government, that recovery is likely, will not cause the litigation fund to continue funding the case. At the same time, a pure litigation funder will face limits on its ability to control the conduct of the litigation because the attorney has ethical duties to the client state. When a person hires an attorney, that attorney has a duty to put the interests of his client first and follow the instructions of the client, and so the attorney that is appointed to manage the case will still take instructions from the government. Nevertheless, as stated above, the funder could withdraw its financial assistance if the case is not progressing in the manner it would like. If the attorney is

---

8. Interview with Harbour Litigation Funding, a funding company located in London, U.K., in *Barriers to Asset Recovery: Is Litigation Funding One Solution?* http://www.anticorruptionlaw.com/blog.aspx?entry=5025.

FIGURE 2.3 For-Profit Litigation Funding for States in Asset Recovery Cases

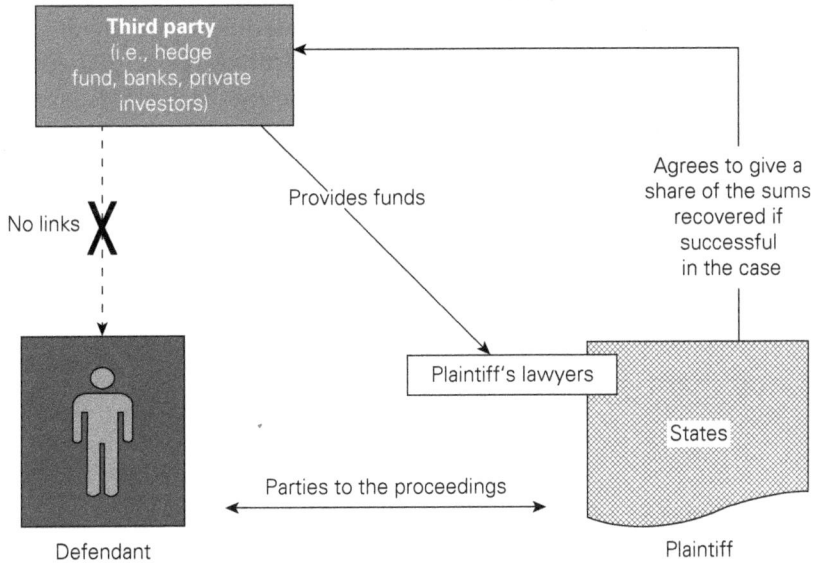

Source: World Bank.

not being paid, they may cease work on the case and formally withdraw from court proceedings.

Thus, as tempting as it may seem, this type of legal financing may involve risks. In addition, the involvement of such funds may not be viable, especially based on possible reputational concerns or inability to manage the process. Government actors should therefore consider the political consequences and costs-benefits analysis associated with this option, as litigation funds take another slice of stolen assets recovered. Furthermore, some jurisdictions have simply prohibited the recourse to litigation funds.

D. Assistance from International Organizations

Some international organizations may offer funding assistance. For instance, the African Legal Support Facility (ALSF), hosted by the African Development Bank, provides assistance to African countries to strengthen their legal expertise and also grants and advances funds to them for legal advice from top legal counsel in these areas. Membership in the ALSF is open to all sovereign nations and international organizations. The facility currently has 52 members, comprising 47 countries and five international organizations. For example, the ALSF has been supporting the Tunisian government in hiring attorneys and covering part of the cost of civil and criminal asset recovery litigation launched after the fall of former president Ben Ali's regime.

The Stolen Asset Recovery Initiative, or StAR, a partnership between the World Bank Group and the United Nations Office on Drugs and Crime (UNODC), strongly supports international efforts to end safe havens for corrupt funds. StAR works with developing countries and financial centers to prevent the laundering of proceeds of corruption and to facilitate a more systematic and timely return of stolen assets.[9] Although it does not offer funding or civil litigation services, StAR can be approached for assistance and advice in accordance with its mandate.

9. See the StAR initiative website, http://star.worldbank.org/star/.

3. Choice of Forum: Where to Sue?

At the outset, countries must consider where to bring the claim, as that may determine which lawyers to hire (based on local expertise), whether the civil action will actually lead to recovery of assets, and how quickly a claim may be brought. Countries and their counsel need to confer early and often about where lawsuits should be brought. The decision is of fundamental importance, and the choice of a jurisdiction is as decisive as the choice of types of claim, or "cause of action" in legal parlance. Past experience indicates that the main factors to consider are often where the assets are located and where defendants have contacts. Other elements, such as the state whose laws will apply and other pending civil or criminal actions, are also at play, as explored below.

A. Where Are the Assets, and Where Do the Defendants Have Contacts?

To reiterate, where to sue is a matter of great importance for potential plaintiffs. In weighing the options, it is essential to consider a number of factors. As we shall see, the decision where to sue may be heavily influenced by where the corruptly acquired assets are located. General considerations include the following: Does the court have jurisdiction? Are there any multilateral or bilateral treaties in place that provide for obtaining evidence? and Would the relevant countries be willing to provide legal assistance with respect to service of documents, collection of evidence, and enforcement of a judgment?

Before an action is filed, the injured state must seek to determine whether the court where the action would be filed has jurisdiction.[1] The concept of jurisdiction means the power to decide on a certain subject matter and to assert power over certain persons and things. More than one court may have jurisdiction. Where to sue will be limited by which courts in which countries have those powers. To exercise authority and issue binding decisions, a court must have subject matter jurisdiction (also known as competence) or *in rem* jurisdiction with regard to property and personal jurisdiction, that is, the ability to determine the rights of the persons and property involved.[2] In addition, even where those requirements are met, there may be limits on whether that court is the

---

1. Jean-Pierre Brun, Clive Scott, Kevin M. Stephenson, and Larissa Gray, *Asset Recovery Handbook: A Guide for Practitioners* (Washington, DC: World Bank, 2011), 29, http://star.worldbank.org/star/publication/asset-recovery-handbook.
2. To secure personal jurisdiction, the defendant must be properly put on notice of the proceedings. If the defendant in a corruption case is elusive, a court may order notice to his lawyers or agents. Examples include the Abacha and Dariye cases brought in the United Kingdom against Nigerian defendants. See Mark Pieth, ed., *Recovering Stolen Assets* (Bern: Peter Lang, 2008), 249. If the defendant is properly notified and chooses to ignore the action, a judgment in favor of the state may follow quickly.

proper place, known as the "forum," for the lawsuit or whether another place is better. Courts may be reluctant to assert jurisdiction over defendants without a stake in resolving the matter before the court. The case discussed in box 3.1 illustrates the application of some of these principles.

In general, a lawsuit can be brought in the places connected with the events, persons, and property to which the claims relate. The connections need not be extensive and are

BOX 3.1	Case with Assets Located in the United Kingdom and Rejection of the Argument That the Home Country of the Official Is More Appropriate: *Federal Republic of Nigeria v. Joshua Dariye & Another* (United Kingdom)

From May 1999 to May 2007, Joshua Dariye was the governor of Plateau state in the Federal Republic of Nigeria. During his administration, Dariye allegedly misappropriated more than US$11.9 million. Nigeria learned that some of the money was used to purchase property in London, and some was funneled into bank accounts in the United Kingdom and Nigeria.[a] Dariye left office in 2006.

In 2005 and 2007, in the United Kingdom, the Federal Republic of Nigeria initiated two civil actions to confiscate Dariye's ill-gotten assets. Eventually judgment was successfully obtained in both cases.[b] In *Federal Republic of Nigeria v. Dariye & Another*, Dariye challenged the jurisdiction of the court, arguing that Nigeria was a more appropriate forum. The court rejected Dariye's challenge for three main reasons.

First, delay and lack of good faith on the part of Dariye. The court found that his motion appeared to be a delaying tactic rather than a good faith challenge. The court noted that although Dariye, through his attorneys, asked to bring the proceedings to Nigeria, nobody knew where he was and he was believed to be in hiding from the Nigerian authorities.[c] Hence the doubts that his application was made in good faith. The court observed that it was strange that Dariye had asked to transfer proceedings to Nigeria, where he considered himself to be in personal physical danger.[d]

Second was the location of witnesses. Dariye argued that he was entitled to have the proceedings brought against him in Nigeria because many witnesses would only be available for giving oral evidence in Nigeria. The court rejected that argument because it had not been shown that bringing witnesses from Nigeria would be impossible.[e]

The third reason concerned enforcement of the final judgment. The court examined whether it would be difficult to enforce a judgment obtained in Nigeria in relation to bank accounts in England.[f] The court found that it would be impossible for a Nigerian court to obtain disclosure from English banks, and therefore the United Kingdom was the proper forum.[g]

(continued next page)

During the litigation, Nigeria was able to get an order from the United Kingdom court ordering disclosure to Nigeria of information gathered during a criminal investigation by United Kingdom authorities, when the authorities did not oppose and affirmed that disclosure would not prejudice their investigations.[h]

Notes: Federal Republic of Nigeria v. Dariye & Another 2007 WL 919418, at § 16.
a. Asset Recovery Knowledge Center, Joshua Chibi Dariye, http://www.assetrecovery.org/kc/node/44186379-8580-11dd-81c3-399112e3d573.9.
b. Ibid., http://www.assetrecovery.org/kc/node/44186379-8580-11dd-81c3-399112e3d573.4.
c. Ibid. at §15.
d. Ibid.
e. Ibid. at § 8.
f. Ibid. at § 9.
g. Ibid. at §13.
h. See Mark Pieth, ed., *Recovering Stolen Assets*, Basel Institute on Governance (Bern: Peter Lang, 2008), 252.

sometimes called "minimum contacts."[3] In addition, the court must find it reasonable that the action is brought there. The rationale of these limits is that fairness dictates that a person cannot be sued in a place with which he has no contacts, as it would subject the person to extraordinary costs and inconvenience. The diagram in figure 3.1 sets out various considerations.

Although the rules vary from one jurisdiction to another, courts generally have the power to hear proceedings involving corrupt acts causing monetary losses if

- The defendant resides or regularly does business there;
- The defendant has voluntarily consented to the court's jurisdiction (e.g., under contractual arrangements);
- The act of corruption took place there;
- The proceeds of the corrupt acts in question are located or were laundered there; or
- The contract was executed there.[4]

Let us consider further some applications of these principles. In practice, in most jurisdictions, persons can normally be sued where they reside. For example, within the European Union (EU), jurisdiction exists in the EU country in which the defendant is domiciled, regardless of his or her nationality.[5]

---

3. Pieth, *Recovering Stolen Assets*, 246 (concluding that United States and European courts are often "robust in refusing challenges to jurisdiction in corruption cases" and take cases with minor connections to their jurisdictions).
4. Theodore S. Greenberg, Linda M. Samuel, Wingate Grant, and Larissa Gray (StAR), *Stolen Asset Recovery—A Good Practices Guide for Non-Conviction Based Asset Forfeiture* (Washington, DC: World Bank, 2009), 122, discussing United Kingdom courts.
5. See new Article 4 of the Regulation of the European Parliament and of the Council amending Regulation (EU) No. 1215/2012, of December 12, 2012, which will enter into force on January 10, 2015.

FIGURE 3.1 Considerations for Where to File a Lawsuit

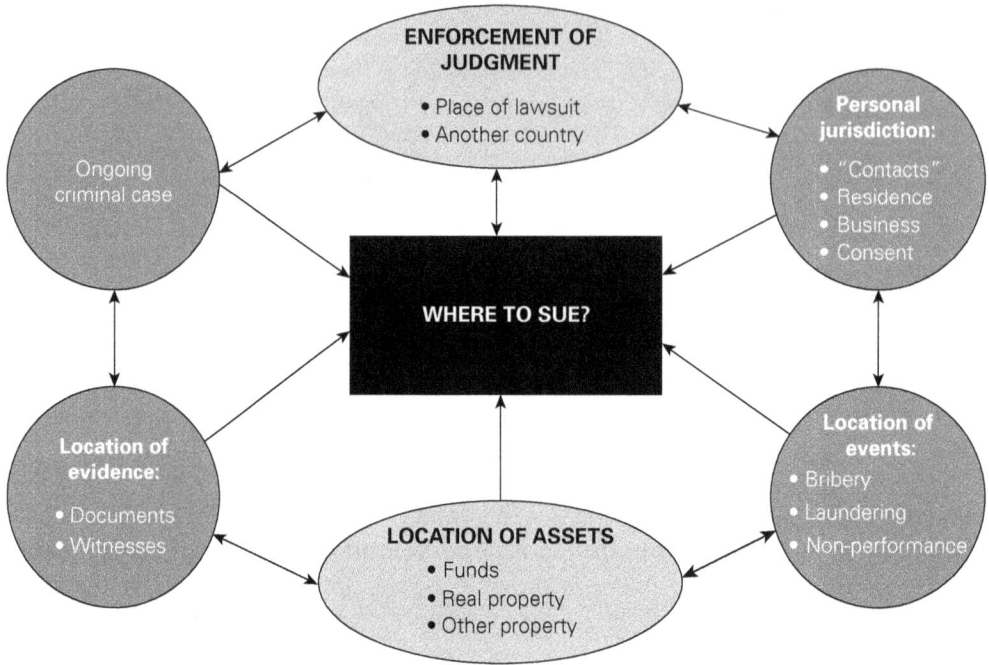

Source: World Bank.

Most important in some jurisdictions, a person can be sued in the place where his assets are located—property that he owns or over which he exercises control, especially if those assets relate to the lawsuit. The European Union provides a good example for claims based on property by going further and allowing exclusive jurisdiction, regardless of the domicile of the parties, to courts of the member state in which the immovable property or tenancies of immovable property are situated.[6]

If a judgment is obtained in the place where the assets are located, it will be easy to seize the assets or perhaps to get a judgment for equivalent value out of the defendant's other assets. Courts often have jurisdiction, sometimes exclusively, where real property that is the subject of the dispute is located.[7] For example, in the civil cases against former

---

6. See Article 22 of Regulation (EC) No. 44/2001 or Brussels I Regulation, to be modified by the new Article 24 of the Regulation of the European Parliament and of the Council amending Regulation (EU) No. 1215/2012, of December 12, 2012, that will enter into force on January 10, 2015. There is no substantive change on that provision. Article 24 just provides more explicitly that the existing exclusive jurisdiction rule includes claims regardless of the domicile of the parties, whereas it previously mentioned only "regardless of domicile."

7. For example, see the Brussels regime on Recognition and Enforcement of Judgments in Civil and Commercial Matters Article 22 of Regulation (EC) No. 44/2001 or Brussels I Regulation, soon to be modified by the new Article 24 of the Proposal for a Regulation of the European Parliament and of the Council amending Regulation (EU) No. 1215/2012, of December 12, 2012, that will enter into force on January 10, 2015.

Zambian president Chiluba and his associates, outlined in box 3.2 below, the presence of relevant bank accounts in London was a powerful factor favoring filing suit in the United Kingdom. Besides, many of the defendants had fled Zambia.

Defendants can be expected to challenge the jurisdiction of a court, as that is one of the first avenues toward having a lawsuit dismissed. On rare occasions, although a court

---

BOX 3.2 — **Successful Civil Suits in the U.K. Where the Money Was Located and Laundered: The Case of Frederick Chiluba (Zambia)**

This case is discussed in box 1.9, in chapter 1, in connection with Zambia's attempts to hold law firms liable for concealing proceeds. Although that part of the litigation was ultimately unsuccessful, another civil lawsuit against Chiluba and his associates yielded substantial asset recovery.

As noted, Chiluba left the presidency in 2002. In February 2003, he was criminally charged in Zambia—along with his former intelligence chief, Xavier Chungu, and several officials—with 168 counts of misappropriation and laundering of more than US$40 million in state funds. The allegations involved assets that were diverted from the Ministry of Finance into an account held at the London branch of the Zambia National Commercial Bank (Zanaco). The Zambian government claimed that the account was used to meet Chiluba's personal expenses, and the defendant argued that the account was used by Zambia's intelligence services to fund operations abroad.[a] Chiluba was eventually acquitted in the criminal case.

In 2004, in the United Kingdom, the attorney general of Zambia, for and on behalf of the Republic of Zambia, brought a civil case against Chiluba and 19 of his associates to recover sums that were transferred by the Ministry of Finance between 1995 and 2001. The money in question was allegedly transferred in payment of debts owed by the government. The attorney general of Zambia acknowledged that some money was indeed used for such purpose but most of it was not.[b] In 2007, the U.K. court found Chiluba and his codefendants liable for misappropriating US$46 million. Thus Zambia won a large damage award.

Bringing the action in London had some advantages because of the close nexus of assets and defendants with London. Much of the allegedly stolen money was transferred through or held in accounts in London.[c] Most of the funds diverted from Zambia had passed through law firms and bank accounts in the United Kingdom.[d] In addition, a number of individual defendants had close ties with London.[e] Finally, the judgments were easily and immediately enforceable without further legal action.

Notes: Attorney General of Zambia v. Meer Care & Desai *(a firm)* & Ors., [2007] EWHC 952, at § 1. For more information on the legal theories of the case, see box 1.9 in chapter 1 (Zamtrop conspiracy case).
a. Asset Recovery Knowledge Center, Frederick Chiluba, http://www.assetrecovery.org/kc/node/4ec2e572-cd77-11dc-b471-db7db47931e5.108.
b. Ibid.
c. Ibid. at § 15.
d. Jean-Pierre Brun, Clive Scott, Kevin M. Stephenson, and Larissa Gray, *Asset Recovery Handbook: A Guide for Practitioners* (Washington, DC: World Bank, 2011), 17, http://star.worldbank.org/star/publication/asset-recovery-handbook.
e. Ibid., 16.

has power over a case, it may also decline to hear it for reasons linked to international immunity of officials or on "prudential" grounds.[8]

As noted above, a case should be dismissed when the court does not have personal or specific jurisdiction on a civil case. On one hand, defendants will often argue that they have no ties to the place of the court. On the other hand, if a party fails to appear in court or contest a claim, the state claimant may win by default. The example in box 3.3 illustrates both of these points.

In addition, defendants may challenge jurisdiction on the grounds that another court is the more appropriate forum, known in Latin as *forum non conveniens*.[9]

Ease of enforcing a judgment is a factor favoring a court's agreeing to hear a case, as illustrated by the *Dariye* decision discussed above. Conversely, if the person does not have assets in the jurisdiction where the lawsuit is brought, the claimant may have to

---

8. See discussion on *forum non conveniens* in note 9, concerning the Piper Aircraft case.
9. The Supreme Court of the United States recognized this doctrine in Piper Aircraft v. Reyno, 454 U.S. 235, 250 (1981), holding that the U.S. court can decline to exercise jurisdiction over a case where a foreign tribunal can more appropriately conduct the litigation.

Winning a Substantial Amount through Settlement in the United States: *Alba v. Alcoa Company* (United States)

In 2008 Alba, which is the state-owned entity (SOE) in Bahrain responsible for aluminum purchases, sued Alcoa Company in U.S. federal court. The allegation was that Alcoa had engaged in a bribery scheme to win lucrative contracts with Bahrain. Alcoa used shell companies to extract inflated payments for aluminum from Alba, then used part of those payments to pay kickbacks, including payments to members of the Bahrain royal family. In 2012, Alcoa paid US$85 million to the Bahrain SOE Alba, to settle the suit out of court.

Note: Alcoa admitted and confirmed this settlement on its website: http://www.alcoa.com/global/en/news/news_detail.asp?pageID=20140109000182en&newsYear=2014.

take his judgment to courts in another jurisdiction and ask them to enforce the order of the first court. That is often more difficult and costly.[10]

Assuming jurisdiction exists, there is always the possibility to reach a settlement with the defendants. Many defendants will want to end the litigation and may be willing to pay substantial sums to settle the claim. In many cases the disputing parties will choose to settle the matter before or during the court proceedings. Both sides typically have a strong incentive to settle, to avoid the costs (such as fees for lawyers and expert witnesses), time, uncertainty, and stress associated with a trial; to achieve a milder punishment in a parallel criminal law trial or avoid being suspended or debarred; and to maintain some control over the amount of the final judgment.[11] Authorities should verify that settlements do not include a waiver of future claims related to assets that were not fully disclosed at the time of the agreement. The case described in box 3.4 is an illustration.

B. Further Considerations

Even if the court is willing to accept jurisdiction, further issues must be considered. They include the choice of law to be applied; whether other criminal or civil actions are pending; the risk of loss of immunities; and whether arbitration is a possibility for some or all of the claims.

Choice of Law

The law on a particular issue can vary significantly from one country to another. Filing your claim where the law is favorable may be important, as it may determine the success

---

10. See chapter 8, "Enforcement and Collection of Judgments."
11. See StAR publication, J. Oduor, F. Fernando, A. Flah, D. Gottwald, J. Hauch, M. Mathias, J. Park, and O. Stolpe, *Left Out of the Bargain: Settlements in Foreign Bribery Cases and Implications for Asset Recovery* (Washington, DC: World Bank, 2013).

A Russian shipping company sued its former senior officers in the courts of the United Kingdom for dishonestly entering into certain shipping transactions that were against the interests of the principal. It was alleged that two of the former officers received bribes.

The issue was whether Russian or English law applied. If the court decided that Russian law applied, then the claims concerning bribery would fail because under Russian law a bribe is not recoverable if the claimant cannot show any loss (because there is no principle of accounting for profit). If the court applied English law, however, there would be an irrefutable presumption that transactions were entered into as a result of bribes and a further irrefutable presumption that there was loss, at least in the amount of the bribes. At first instance, among other things, the judge found that bribes were paid in the amount of about US$350,000, but because Russian law applied, the judge dismissed that part of the claim.

The appellate court reexamined whether English or Russian law governed, and it affirmed the choice of Russian law, causing the company to lose. The court of appeal relied on the Private International Law (Miscellaneous Provisions Act 1998), citing a number of factors pointing to Russian law as the governing law, including the place where the events constituting the tort took place and where the harm was sustained. In this case all the elements of the tort took place in Russia, particularly the promise and arrangements for any bribe. The fact that Russian law was applicable was fatal for that part of the claim.

Note: Fiona Trust & Holding Corp. & Ors. v. Dimitri Skarga & Ors. [2013] EWCA Civ 275 (March 26, 2013).

or failure of your claim. However, even though a court accepts jurisdiction over a case, it does not mean that the court will necessarily apply the law of its country. It is possible for a court to decide that a foreign law governs the claim, which could have a decisive impact on the outcome, as illustrated in the case described in box 3.5.

Other Criminal Action Already Pending

The choice of where to initiate a civil action may also be influenced by where a criminal action is already pending. If the defendant is already being prosecuted in a criminal action, courts of that country may be an additional option for a civil action.[12] Some jurisdictions, however, may suspend civil actions until the criminal case is resolved.[13]

---

12. Under Article 5 paragraph 4 of the Brussels I Regulation, one can bring a civil claim for damages or restitution which is based on an act giving rise to criminal proceedings, in the court hearing the criminal case, to the extent that that court has jurisdiction under its own law to entertain civil proceedings, as long as the defendant has a domicile in any of the states party to the convention.

13. See chapter 4, under the subhead "Civil Actions Based on Criminal Actions."

In parallel, in civil law jurisdictions, if a criminal case is pending, a "state victim" may have the right to participate as a civil party in the criminal action and may wish to explore that avenue as a means of asserting a claim for monetary damages.[14]

Other Civil Lawsuit Already Pending

Filing a lawsuit may limit options to file future suits against the same parties. In cases where a second lawsuit is filed about the same matter, by the same parties, in a different court, the subsequent courts may defer to the first court and dismiss the second action. This principle is embodied in Article 21 of the Brussels I Regulation, which provides that "where proceedings involving the same cause of action and between the same parties are brought in the courts of different Contracting States, any court other than the court first seized shall decline jurisdiction in favor of that court."[15]

The Interplay of Local and Foreign Proceedings

Considering foreign courts when determining the choice of forum can prove effective. In the event that the criminal procedure before local courts is lengthy, a civil action in the jurisdiction where the assets are located—or even participation as a civil party in a criminal procedure abroad—can be the only opportunity to recover the assets, especially if the mutual legal assistance request based on the local criminal action is not likely to succeed. In addition, in some jurisdictions, particularly the democratic transition regimes, local authorities might not be able to prepare a suitable mutual legal assistance request to seek the recovery of assets abroad because of lack of evidence against former high-level officials. Notwithstanding, law enforcement authorities in the jurisdiction where the assets are located are generally able to launch criminal action against the same persons, based on bank reports and other evidence collected there. In that situation appearance as a civil party before the foreign court can help the victim states to collect the evidence needed to prepare later a suitable request for mutual legal assistance.

When There Is Exclusive Jurisdiction

The decision to initiate a civil action abroad should be consistent with domestic rules regarding the exercise of jurisdiction by local courts. The decision should not contravene the exclusive exercise of jurisdiction by local courts, where domestic laws provide for it. Such a violation would normally not entail any implications before the foreign court (since it will only assess its own grounds for performing jurisdiction), but the enforcement of a future judgment in the jurisdiction of the victim state—if necessary—would probably be denied.

---

14. See chapter 1, under the subhead "States and Government Entities as Civil Party in Criminal Proceedings," and chapter 4, under "Civil Actions Based on Criminal Actions."

15. The Lugano Convention on Jurisdiction and the Enforcement of Judgments in Civil and Commercial Matters, OJ L 339, 21.12.2007 (88/592/EEC, 1988) has a similar provision at Article 27.

Sovereign Immunities and the Risk of Potential Counterclaims

Another interesting element to consider when states and government entities envisage civil litigation in a foreign jurisdiction is the risk of being exposed to potential counterclaims arising out of the same legal relationship or facts as the principal claim. The principle that a sovereign state cannot be sued in the courts of a foreign state is a well-established rule under customary international law. The immunity from the jurisdiction of the forum state, however, is rarely absolute. States may waive their immunity or consent to suit. They can do so explicitly, by enacting legislation, or implicitly by exercising their right to sue.[16] In that situation, suing may extinguish certain immunities. The issue of potential counterclaims appears at a domestic level but is even more relevant when the choice of forum includes a foreign jurisdiction. Therefore, the choice of a foreign jurisdiction, and the consequent reduction or waiver of immunity from the foreign jurisdiction, should be well thought out and decided by competent authorities in the plaintiff (victim) state.[17]

Forums beyond the Courts—Arbitration

To complete the discussion of forums for dispute resolution with respect to state contracts, it should be noted that arbitration clauses may be included in contracts related to international investments. In such cases, one must consider another possibility, which most likely would arise in situations where a state cancels a contract and refuses to pay based on allegations of corruption. Then parties may seek, or be obliged, to settle the dispute outside the courts, through a process called arbitration.[18] Arbitration proceedings related to international contracts obtained through bribes or through illicit advantages awarded to corrupt officials may open promising avenues, including the cancellation of contracts and potential claims for torts or damages. Examples of disputes arising from international investment contracts are discussed later in this book, including the discussions in box 4.7, in chapter 4, concerning *World Duty Free Company Limited v. The Republic of Kenya* (2006), and box 7.4, in chapter 7, regarding *Cameroon Airlines v Transnet Ltd.* (2004).

---

16. See for example, in the United States, the Foreign Sovereign Immunities Act of 1976.

17. In Brazil, for instance, this decision belongs to the attorney general of the union, by delegation of the president of the republic, to authorize the appearance of Brazil before foreign courts (Decree n. 7.598/2010).

18. Arbitration is a procedure in which the parties agree to resolve a dispute by submitting it to one or more private persons who have no financial interest in the outcome. Arbitration can be used when an international contract provides an arbitration clause or when a bilateral investment treaty provides a basis for investment arbitration. The majority of bilateral investment treaties provide either for mandatory dispute resolution mechanisms or for recourse to international arbitration under the auspices of the International Centre for the Settlement of Investment Disputes (ICSID).

4. Types of Actions

A plaintiff state has a choice of legal theories on which to base its claims. The state may have either a *proprietary* claim, to enforce its ownership rights on a particular identifiable asset, or a *personal* claim, against a particular person or entity for damages or restitution (see figure 4.1).

The advantage of a proprietary claim is that it is enforceable independent of the status of other creditors. As we shall see, the common law offers a wider array of options to exercise proprietary claims, whereas for personal claims common and civil law systems offer similar options. We shall first consider proprietary claims and then move on to various types of personal claims, such as torts, breach of contract, and restitution based on unjust enrichment.

A. Proprietary Actions—State Asserts Claim to a Particular Asset

A *proprietary* claim is a claim that one owns something and asks the court to return that item or its equivalent value. Under the United Nations Convention Against Corruption (UNCAC), a state, when it is the legitimate owner of an asset, should be able to exercise its full rights to that asset, no matter who has possession of it.[1] That, in a nutshell, is the idea underlying proprietary actions under both civil and common law systems. The difference lies in the way that ownership is understood. The slightly more differentiated understanding of ownership under common law allows for a wider variety of legal action.

1. Proprietary Actions under Common Law

Definition and examples of proprietary claims
Historically English courts have ruled that a defrauded principal (i.e., the state) that is the victim of embezzlement or misappropriation of funds is the "beneficial owner" of those assets. Embezzled and misappropriated state funds qualify as state property and are subject to a proprietary claim. Because the state (the defrauded principal) is considered the owner of the property in question, his claim extends not only to the property in question but also to any profits that may have derived from it. In addition, it does not extend only to the property itself but also to any subsequent assets into which the original property may have been converted. This legal point takes on great importance because corrupt actors frequently engage in many transactions to hide stolen assets.

---

1. See UNCAC, Articles 53 to 55.

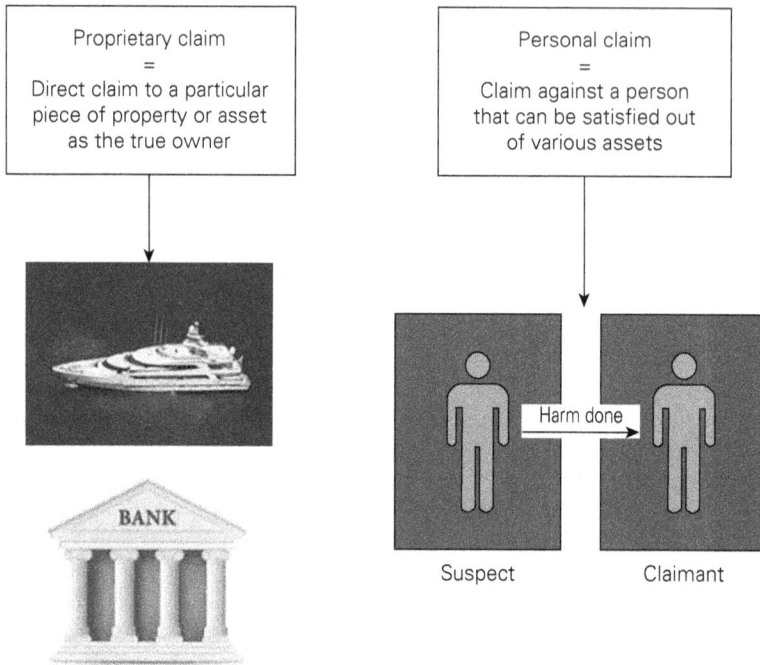

FIGURE 4.1 Types of Claims without Links and with Harm Done Illustrated

| Proprietary claim
=
Direct claim to a particular
piece of property or asset
as the true owner | Personal claim
=
Claim against a person
that can be satisfied out
of various assets |

Harm done

Suspect   Claimant

Source: World Bank.

The beneficial interest of the defrauded principal remains attached to the asset along the way if the claimant can "trace" it. "Tracing" is the process by which "a claimant demonstrates what has happened to his property, identifies its proceeds and justifies his claim that the proceeds can properly be regarded as representing his property."[2] The holder of the beneficial interest can follow that trail and exercise his claim even where there have been numerous successive transactions. His interest binds everyone who takes the property or its traceable proceeds except a bona fide purchaser for value without notice of the breach of trust. A bona fide purchaser is a person who has purchased an asset for stated value, innocent of any fact which would cast doubt on the right of the seller to have sold it in good faith. If the true owner shows up to claim title to the asset, the bona fide purchaser will in some jurisdictions be able to retain the asset, and the real owner will have to seek compensation from the fraudulent seller. However, regarding the bona fide purchaser, certain differences between legal systems should be underlined. Civil law countries (for example, in Switzerland, Japan, or Germany) may protect bona fide purchasers, which protection will prevail for a certain period from the date of the theft. Meanwhile, and specifically in common law countries, a subsequent bona fide

---

2. Foskett v. McKeown and others [2001] 1 A.C. 102 (H.L.) (Eng.) (describing tracing as neither a claim nor a remedy but merely a "process").

State Recovers Property Bought with State Funds:
***State of Libya v. Capitana Seas Ltd.* (United Kingdom)**

In December 2011, the state of Libya brought an action in the High Court in London to obtain ownership of a £10 million house in London belonging to Capitana Seas Limited (Capitana), a British Virgin Islands company ultimately controlled by Saadi Qadafi, the son of the former ruler of Libya, Muammer Qadafi. Neither Saadi Qadafi nor Capitana appeared in court to defend the proceedings. Counsel for Libya then moved for a default judgment.

In March 2012, the judge found that state funds had been used to obtain the property and ruled, "I am satisfied, on the evidence which has been put before me, that Saadi Qadafi is the sole ultimate beneficial owner of the Defendant company [Capitana]. I am satisfied, on the evidence before me, that the property was wrongfully and unlawfully purchased with funds belonging to the Claimant [Libya]. In those circumstances, the beneficial interest in the property is held by the Defendant, for the Claimant, as constructive trustee." The judge thus awarded the property to claimant country, Libya.

The case was relatively straightforward as the house was known to belong to Saadi Qadafi, and the U.K. Treasury sanctions list stated that Saadi was the owner of Capitana, and therefore of the house. Following the court's order, the U.K. Treasury consented to the action, permitting transfer of the property to Libya.

Note: See case description at http://star.worldbank.org/corruption-cases/node/19587; http://www.thebureauinvestigates.com/2012/03/09/saadi-gaddafi-ordered-by-high-court-to-hand-over-10m-london-house-to-people-of-libya/; and http://www.anticorruptionlaw.com/blog.aspx?entry=5238.

purchaser may not acquire ownership of the stolen property because a stolen asset cannot convey good title.

A few examples, in boxes 4.1 and 4.2, illustrate how courts may grant the state's request to return assets to it, if there is enough evidence to conclude that the source of the funds used to acquire the assets is the state.

The courts of the United Kingdom employed similar reasoning to the Qadafi case in a case concerning Nigerian official Alamieyeseigha, as illustrated in box 4.2.

Proprietary Claims and Bribes

The same notion of property and beneficial ownership may extend further to bribes paid to an official in furtherance of obtaining a certain contract. Several court decisions (see below) show how bribes, and property purchased by using them, qualified as property to which the state holds beneficial title, allowing the state to vindicate, as beneficial owner, the repayment of that bribe. As explained later, a recent court decision has cast some uncertainty over this theory.[3] Nonetheless, it may be useful.

---

3. Sinclair Investments v. Versailles Trade Finance Limited (2011) EWCA (iv) 347.

These court decisions were based on the theory of "constructive trust," under which assets acquired as a consequence of a breach of a fiduciary duty (taking bribes) belong to, and are held on behalf of, the party whose trust has been betrayed (the state or the corporation whose agent has been bribed). The cases described in boxes 4.3 and 4.4 illustrate how this theory was used in Hong Kong SAR, China, and Singapore.

Readers should note, however, that the position under English law is now unclear as a result of a number of recent court decisions, most notably the Sinclair Investments case, described in box 4.5, in which the United Kingdom Court of Appeals declined to follow the principles defined in *Attorney General of Hong Kong v. Reid*. In other words, the court in *Reid* ruled that the principal (the state) has a proprietary claim to bribes received by its fiduciary (the official) and thus a claim on increases in value. In contrast, in the Sinclair decision, even though the state may claim the value of the bribe, the court ruled that a principal cannot claim a proprietary interest. By this reasoning, there is no constructive trust, and there may be no claim for any increase in value of assets acquired with a bribe. It is not clear which approach courts will follow.

BOX 4.3

Using "Constructive Trust" to Recover Bribes Paid to a Corrupt Official: *AG of Hong Kong v. Reid* (Hong Kong SAR, China)

Charles Warwick Reid, a lawyer from New Zealand, arrived in Hong Kong to join the Attorney General's Chambers in 1975 and eventually worked his way up to principal crown counsel and the head of Hong Kong's Commercial Crime Unit. By 1989, he had acquired control of assets amounting to roughly HK$12.4 million, inexplicably and disproportionately to his earnings. In October 1989, Reid was suspended from duty and arrested by Hong Kong's independent counsel against corruption (ICAC) on suspicion of corruption.

The attorney general of Hong Kong was forced to fight a precedent-setting battle all the way up to the Judicial Committee of the Privy Council in London. The steps were necessary to recover the portions of the approximately HK$12.4 million of bribe money that had been converted into property after passing through various corporate vehicles and legal owners in New Zealand on Reid's behalf.

The issue at stake was that the government of Hong Kong maintained that it held an interest in the Reid-owned properties in New Zealand, as they represented the proceeds of bribery while Reid was in dereliction of his fiduciary duties as a civil servant. The Privy Council judgment took for granted that the New Zealand properties were purchased with Reid's bribe money. The Privy Council judgment was based on the principle of equity, which considers "as done that which ought to have been done."

The council determined that the assets received by Reid as bribe payments should have been "paid or transferred to the person who suffered from the breach of duty." This point is of great consequence to the legal relationship held between the bribe-receiving fiduciary and the party whose trust has been betrayed; it provides a means of redress. As a result of the Privy Council ruling, English common law (and many other legal systems) recognized that property acquired in breach of trust belongs in equity to the beneficiary (in legal terms, the *cestui que* trust); in other words, persons holding such property do so in constructive trust for the true owner. It also held that if the value of the property representing the bribe depreciated, the fiduciary had to pay the injured person the difference between that value and the initial amount of the bribe. If the property increased in value, the fiduciary was not entitled to retain the excess since equity would not allow him to make any profit from his breach of duty.[a]

Notes: AG for Hong Kong v. Reid [1993] UKPC 2 (November 1, 1993) [1994] 1 All ER 1, [1993] UKPC 2, [1994] AC 324, [1994] 1 AC 324, http://www.bailii.org/uk/cases/UKPC/1993/2.html.
a. Emile van der Does de Willebois, Emily Halter, Robert Harrison, Ji Won Park, and J. C. Sharman, *The Puppet Masters—How the Corrupt Use Legal Structures to Hide Stolen Assets and What to Do about It* (Washington, DC: World Bank, 2011), 175.

BOX 4.4	Successful Proprietary Claim to Recover Bribes: More on *Kartika Ratna Thahir v. Pertamina* (Singapore)

The basic facts of this case are set out in box 1.5, in chapter 1. Pertamina, an Indonesian state-owned energy enterprise (SOE), sued its former executive Haji Thahir to recover bribes he received from two contractors hoping for better contractual terms and preferential treatment. Thahir had deposited the bribes into a bank in Singapore. In determining whether the SOE Pertamina had a proprietary claim on the funds in the account, the court found that Thahir owed a fiduciary duty to Pertamina and that the bribes he received were held as a constructive trustee for the company, meaning that the SOE held a proprietary claim to the money.

Note: See case description at http://star.worldbank.org/corruption-cases/sites/corruption-cases/files/documents/arw /Pertamina_Singapore_Appeals_Court_Aug_25_1994.pdf.

BOX 4.5	Discussion on the Reasoning of *Hong Kong v. Reid: Sinclair Investments v. Versailles*

The Sinclair case involved a breach of fiduciary duty but not an actual bribe. The court of appeal held that the beneficiary of a fiduciary duty cannot claim proprietary rights unless the assets were previously its property, or unless the agent (here, the public official) who breached the fiduciary duty acquired the assets by taking advantage of a right or an opportunity of the beneficiary. If one applies this reasoning to the situation of bribes, it would mean that the state, as the beneficiary of a fiduciary duty, would encounter difficulty in claiming its proprietary rights. First, the bribes and secret commissions paid by the briber to a corrupt official clearly were not previously its property. Second, in some cases, it may be difficult to show that the public official (the agent) acquired the right or opportunity of the beneficiary. As a result, whether secret commissions or bribes are recoverable on a proprietary basis will be largely dependent on the particular facts of the case until the matter is clarified by the courts or legislatures.

The Jersey Royal Court, for example, chose in November 2013 to follow and apply *Reid.* It found that a trustee who held funds constituting the proceeds of bribery of an official in Mozambique did so as a constructive trustee for the government of Mozambique, which thus held a proprietary claim to the funds.[a]

Notes: Sinclair Investments (U.K.) Ltd. v. Versailles Trade Finance Ltd., [2011] EWCA Civ 347, March 29, 2011, http://www.bailii.org /ew/cases/EWCA/Civ/2011/347.html.
a. David Wilson, Baker and Partners, "Jersey: Jersey Court Endorses Proprietary Claim to Proceeds of Corruption in re The Representation of Lloyds TSB Offshore Trust Company Limited," 2013, http://www.mondaq.com/x/273702/Trusts/Jersey+Court +Endorses+Proprietary+Claim+To+Proceeds+Of+Corruption+In+Re+The+Representation+Of+Lloyds+TSB+Offshore+Trust+C ompany+Limited. The case can be found at http://www.jerseylaw.je/Judgments/UnreportedJudgments/Documents/Display .aspx?url=2013/13-10-31_Rep_of_Lloyds_Trust_Co_(CI)_Ltd_211.htm&JudgementNo=%5B2013%5DJRC211.

2. Claiming Back Property—A Limited Right in Civil Law Systems

Most civil law systems also provide for an action to claim back one's property as the owner of that property.[4] The right can be exercised against anyone holding that property, with exceptions for bona fide acquirers. Those causes of action in civil law countries, however, tend to be limited in scope to the return of the thing (*res*) itself (i.e., there is no tracing of the asset through changes in form), are sometimes limited in time, and rarely extend to profits generated by the asset. Tracing is fundamental, as the assets and the proceeds must be clearly identified before they can be subject to a proprietary claim. Typically, tracing sums of money as such is intricate, making it difficult to be the subject of a proprietary action under civil law. Money (notably cash) is totally fungible and hence not easily identifiable, but in some cases that obstacle has been overcome (see box 4.6).

There is thus some marginal precedent for a proprietary action to seek the return of funds under civil law. However, in civil law countries, where proprietary actions based on a constructive trust do not exist, plaintiffs still have the option to base their action on personal claims instead to recover the funds.

BOX 4.6   Claiming Back Funds in Quebec: *Saroglou v. Canada*

The legal system of Quebec is acknowledged to combine elements of common and civil law. The civil (private) law of Quebec is considered to be civil law in nature, whereas public and criminal laws are considered to operate according to common law.

In *Saroglou v. Canada*, a party had a "revendication" claim on a sum of money (that is, the party says the sum of money is hers or his) against many defendants, among them the receiver general, a public authority. The claimant sought to recover the asset on the basis of a real claim. The defendant pointed out that the claim was personal. This issue was important to determine the jurisdiction of the court. In deciding whether the action was real or personal, the judge held that as "money is a fungible asset, to be able to claim title to it, it should be clearly identifiable. It is not sufficient that it be [merely] quantifiable" and concluded that "it appears, therefore, that for a claim to lie in regard to a sum of money, certain factual proof must be made concerning the type of accounting and deposit that has been used." Therefore, as long as the money claimed is identifiable, its revendication is a real claim and not a personal one.

Source: World Bank.

---

4. In France, this action is called "*action en revendication*." In Germany, the action is called "*vindikation*" and is a substantive claim granted in § 985 of the civil code.

B. Personal Claims—Claim against a Person

Proprietary claims and remedies will not be available in all cases. For instance, they may not be available if the proceeds cannot be traced because they have been successfully laundered, so as to render it impossible to make a link between the original funds and the funds ultimately identified in the defendant's estate. In that case, a personal claim may be brought against persons holding the assets in question or those who have participated in the corrupt act or the ensuing money laundering. In contrast to asserting that the plaintiff state is the true owner (or proprietor) of a property, the state can claim, for example, that it has suffered economic damages and demand to be paid or compensated by the person who caused the damage. This is a personal claim. Other examples of such claims include breach or annulment of contract, tort, and unjust enrichment.

1. Contracts

In many cases of corruption, a contractual relationship will exist between the state and the perpetrator of the corrupt act. For bribery, the situation that most readily comes to mind is that of an employment contract between a principal (the state) and his agent (the bribe taker) or a contract for the performance of work between a state and a private company (the bribe payer).[5] Where embezzlement is concerned, as in bribery, the embezzler will often be in some way employed by, or performing certain services for, the harmed party.

Actions Based on Invalidity of Contracts
If the state can show that a contract is invalid or that the other party breached the contract, it can seek monetary damages or contractual restitution or can refuse to enforce the contract. Invalidity may be based on the grounds that the contract was extorted by fraud and that consent was vitiated by corruption.

Regarding invalidity of the contract, a distinction has to be made between the primary agreement (or "contract") involving the payment of the bribe or other offenses and the secondary contract obtained through corruption. The primary agreement that is tainted by illegality is often considered null and void, and thus unenforceable. The illegality of the agreement is generally rooted in the social harm caused by corruption and the violation of general moral principles, rather than on the quantified actual damages to the aggrieved party. The "main contract," a public contract or a clause of a contract obtained through corruption, may also be considered void and without any legal effect on grounds

---

5. The agreement to pay the bribe, of course, generally invalid *ob turpem causam* (cf. Article 8 paragraph 1 of the Council of Europe Civil Law Convention on Corruption: "Each party shall provide in its internal law for any contract or clause of a contract providing for corruption to be null and void."). This is also the rule in the list of transnational principles "TRANS-LEX," published by the Center of Transnational Law. Under IV.7.2(a), "Contracts based on or involving the payment or transfer of bribes ("corruption money," "secret commissions," "pots-de-vin," "kickbacks") are void." Available at http://www.trans-lex.org/output .php?docid=938000.

of public policy. As an example, Kenya requested an arbitral tribunal to declare unenforceable an agreement obtained by bribing a government official (box 4.7).[6]

In some other jurisdictions, a contract obtained by fraud is not void but voidable.[7] The state is entitled to rescind the contract, particularly in cases of bribery and collusion in bidding.[8] A claim for rescission may require proof that the government entity would have refused the contract in the absence of any fraudulent act. The state may still wish to enforce the contract derived from the bribe if, for example, execution is already too far advanced or the provider has proprietary or unique goods or services. In that case, damages may consist of the excess amount paid by the state under the contract. The government entity would then be entitled to damages for entering the contract

---

6. Another example in California, in Adler v. Federal Republic of Nigeria,19 February 1997, 107 F.3d 720 (9th Cir. 1997), the court applied the unclean hands doctrine to bar the plaintiff (Adler) from recovering the five million dollars he paid to further the illegal contract and to bribe Nigerian government officials. This decision was confirmed by the Court of Appeal on May 17, 2000 (219 F.3d 869 [9th Cir. 2000]).

7. David Kraft, "English Private Law and Corruption: Summary and Suggestions for the Development of European Private Law," in *The Civil Law Consequences of Corruption,* edited by Olaf Meyer (Baden-Baden: Nomos, 2009).

8. Ross River Ltd. v. Cambridge City Football Club Ltd. [2007] EWHC 2115 (Ch) (U.K.). The case can be found at http://www.bailii.org/ew/cases/EWHC/Ch/2007/2115.html. In addition, French courts have ruled that government entities that entered a contract tainted by corruption are entitled to request annulation or rescission of contracts and/or damages (see *Service Central de Prévention de la Corruption—Rapport 2010*, p. 182, and cases mentioned, at http://www.ladocumentationfrancaise.fr/var/storage/rapports -publics/114000391/0000.pdf).

Star Platinum and related companies sought to develop a resort in the Turks and Caicos Islands. Using several intermediary vehicles, in 2007 principals of Star Platinum made a payment of US$500,000 to a minister of the government. A short time later, the government granted Star Platinum favorable terms for long-term leases on additional property that would enhance the value of the project. The company paid US$3.2 million for the leases, which was a small fraction of their market value. In the court in Turks and Caicos, the attorney general sued Star Platinum, alleging civil bribery, namely, that the money paid to the minister had been a bribe and demanding to rescind the leases.

In June 2013, the court found a very strong probability that the US$500,000 was a bribe and that the leases were the result of the bribe payment. The court ruled that the attorney general could rescind the leases and, in addition, recover the amount of the bribe or damages resulting from the bribe (but not both). Nor was the state required to repay the US$3.2 million that Star Platinum had paid under the tainted lease deal, since a bank had acquired bona fide rights in the property as security for the principal's debts. As a result, the principal was not able to transfer the property back to the state. Had he transferred the property back, he would have been entitled to reimbursement of the price paid.

Source: World Bank.

under less-favorable terms than would have been agreed to in the absence of the act causing the breach. Depending on the legal system, avoidance of the contract can either be retroactive or be limited to the application of the contract in the future. Expenses incurred by the contractor for having to redo a tender process or negotiate a new contract may or may not qualify as damages.

The example described in box 4.8 demonstrates a state's suing, in its own courts, a corrupt company that had won a valuable land concession through payment of a bribe and forcing rescission of the arrangement, including no repayment of the company's investment in the corrupt deal.[9]

Actions Based on Breach of Contract

In public procurement, corruption is increasingly considered as a material breach of contract, particularly in contracts for building infrastructure projects, for the sale of goods, or for the provision of services. The breach of contract may result in poor

---

9. See Laurence Harris, James Maton, and Jamie Humphreys (Edwards Wildman Palmer UK LLP), "Corruption in UK Off-Shore Territories." *Journal of the Commonwealth Lawyers' Association,* http://www.edwardswildman.com/files/upload/2013_Corruption_in_UK_OffShore.pdf.

performance or nonperformance of an obligation, and from defective products causing injuries to others.[10]

The contract itself may provide a basis for an action for breach of contract if it includes anticorruption clauses wherein the contractor promised not to provide any inducements to public officials in connection with the award or performance of the contract. Violation of this particular prohibition gives the government an entitlement to terminate the contract, avoid its own obligations, and claim damages.[11] If liability is found in breach of contract, the plaintiff, as a general rule, may not have to prove causation between the loss and the corrupt act, or the intent or knowledge of the defendant, to obtain contractual damages.

Under certain circumstances, courts may order profits earned from a contract to be disgorged.[12] Even though in principle damages are measured by the plaintiff's loss, not the defendant's gain, some courts have held that if a person breaches a contract, he should not be allowed to profit from that contractual breach. Thus, in suitable cases, the damages for breach of contract may be measured by "the benefit gained by the wrongdoer from the breach."[13] According to the principle of "unjust enrichment," one person should not be permitted to unjustly enrich himself at the expense of another, but should be required to make restitution for property or benefits unjustly received.[14] However, this issue is debated, as most countries do not have such a rule. Boxes 4.9 and 4.10 provide examples in the United Kingdom and Switzerland of the application of these concepts.

Although it is a logical consequence of the principle that no one can profit from his own wrong, the disgorgement of profits is nonetheless not punitive in character—for that there is criminal law. In any event, when legally available, the possibility of taking profits generated by an act of corruption may also deter perpetrators of corruption.

Under certain circumstances, and depending on the legal system, it may be possible to successfully submit a claim both for damages suffered by the plaintiff and for the disgorgement of profits made by the defendant. Thus a state that is the victim of bribery

---

10. Joseph R. Profaizer (Wilmer, Cutler & Pickering), for the 9th International Anti-Corruption Conference, "Effective Use of Legal and Asset-Tracing Remedies for Corruption: Civil Legal Remedies," 1999, http://9iacc.org/papers/day3/ws1/d3ws1_jrprofaizer.html.

11. Jean-Pierre Brun, Clive Scott, Kevin M. Stephenson, and Larissa Gray, *Asset Recovery Handbook: A Guide for Practitioners* (Washington, DC: World Bank, 2011), http://star.worldbank.org/star/publication/asset-recovery-handbook.

12. Disgorgement is the forced return of illegally obtained profits.

13. Lord Nicholls of Birkenhead, in Attorney General v. Blake [2000]: "*The Wrotham Park case* (*Wrotham Park Estate Co Ltd v. Parkside Homes Ltd* [1974] 1 WLR 798), therefore, still shines, rather as a solitary beacon, showing that in contract as well as tort damages are not always narrowly confined to recoupment of financial loss. In a suitable case damages for breach of contract may be measured by the benefit gained by the wrongdoer from the breach. The defendant must make a reasonable payment in respect of the benefit he has gained."

14. Donald Harris, David Campbell, and Roger Halson, *Remedies in Contract and Tort*, 2d ed. (Cambridge: Cambridge University Press, 2005), 231.

Disgorgement of Profits for Breach of Contract: *Attorney General v. Blake* **(United Kingdom)**

Blake was employed as a member of the secret services of the United Kingdom. When he joined the Secret Intelligence Service, Blake expressly agreed in writing that he would not disclose official information, during or after his service, in book form or otherwise. In 1990, he published his autobiography, *No Other Choice*, in which he disclosed a wealth of official information covered by that provision in his contract. The court ruled that even though the Crown had suffered no monetary damages from Blake's disclosures, the profits gained from the publication of the book were to be paid to the United Kingdom as his employer:

> In considering what would be a just response to a breach of Blake's undertaking the court has to take these considerations into account. The undertaking, if not a fiduciary obligation, was closely akin to a fiduciary obligation, where an account of profits is a standard remedy in the event of breach. Had the information which Blake has now disclosed still been confidential, an account of profits would have been ordered, almost as a matter of course. In the special circumstances of the intelligence services, the same conclusion should follow even though the information is no longer confidential. That would be a just response to the breach. I am reinforced in this view by noting that most of the profits from the book derive indirectly from the extremely serious and damaging breaches of the same undertaking committed by Blake in the 1950s. As already mentioned, but for his notoriety as an infamous spy his autobiography would not have commanded royalties of the magnitude [the publisher] agreed to pay.

Note: Attorney General v. Blake [2000] UKHL 45.

may be able to claim both the profits that a party made as a result of the bribe and the damages that it suffered as a result, even though the plaintiff will be able to collect only for one or the other.

2. Tort Claims

A tort is a "civil" (as opposed to criminal) wrong, giving rise to a claim for damages.[15] Damages compensate a plaintiff for loss, injury, or harm directly caused by a breach of duty, including criminal wrongdoing, immoral conduct, or precontractual fault.

Where a corrupt act has occurred, a state plaintiff generally may have to prove that it suffered compensable damage, that the defendant breached a duty, and that there is a causal link between corruption and the damage. To recover from the defendant in some

---

15. A tort may be defined legally as "an act or an omission that causes damage to another person that constitutes a legal ground for the payment of damages, to the person wronged, by the person to whom the act or omission may be attributed."

jurisdictions, general liability statutes simply require the plaintiff to show that an act or omission by the defendant caused the plaintiff's damages.

Legal persons and individuals who directly and knowingly participate in the corrupt act are primarily liable for the damage. Apart from liability of those who directly initiated or committed the act in question, courts may hold liable those who facilitated the corrupt act or failed to take appropriate steps to prevent corruption. That may be the case for lawyers or intermediaries who assisted in corrupt acts or for parent companies and employers who failed to exert appropriate control over their subsidiaries or employees.[16] It may also include banks through which the funds have passed, lawyers whose clients' accounts were used in transferring stolen assets, or trust and company service providers involved in the setting up and management of shell corporations. Such liability may be founded upon their active participation in the tort. Although

---

16. Brun et al., *Asset Recovery Handbook*, http://star.worldbank.org/star/publication/asset-recovery -handbook.

more difficult to prove, it can also be based on their negligence in verifying the origin of funds or the purpose of the transaction, that is to say, a lack of due diligence.[17]

It is impossible to give a complete overview of the types of acts that may qualify as a tort or noncontractual civil wrong, but in the context of corruption, the following are all relevant: civil fraud, tortuous interference with contract or economic advantage, conspiracy to injure, conversion, and, more generally, the breach of a fiduciary duty. Very relevant in the context of corruption is the tort of misappropriation—alleging that the corrupt official or his associates took property of the state for themselves, illustrated in box 4.11.

Civil wrongs may be committed directly by bribe payers and bribe takers or government officials who embezzle funds. In bribery cases, courts in some jurisdictions may consider that a briber and the person receiving the bribe have committed a joint tort, for which the victim is entitled to recover the entire loss from either party.[18] The basic rule for the determination of damages in corruption cases provides that the victim must be placed as close as possible to the situation he would have been in but for the commission of the corrupt act. Thus, all expenses or lost profits caused by the corrupt act must be compensated.[19] Once the bribe is established, there is often an irrefutable presumption that it was given with an intention to induce the agent to act favorably to the payer

---

17. An example is the "blind eye" theory accepted by some United Kingdom courts and the U.S. courts (see the January 2014 case involving the massive Bernard Madoff fraud scheme, in which J. P. Morgan admitted liability and paid a large penalty); "J. P. Morgan Is Penalized $2 Billion over Madoff," *New York Times*, http://dealbook.nytimes.com/2014/01/07/jpmorgan-settles-with-federal-authorities-in-madoff-case/?_php=true&_type=blogs&_r=0.

18. In the United Kingdom, the defendant may then seek contribution from the joint tort under the Civil Liability (Contributions) Act of 1978.

19. For example, according to article 3 of the Council of Europe Civil Law Convention on Corruption, compensation may cover material damage, loss of profits, and nonpecuniary loss. According to the Explanatory Report § 38, the material damage (*damnum emergens*) refers to the actual reduction in the economic situation of the person who has suffered the damage. The loss of profits (*lucrum cessans*) represents the profit that could reasonably have been expected but that was not gained because of the corrupt act.

and, thereafter, unfavorably to the principal. This presumption will be sufficient to prove that the act was affected and influenced by the payment.[20] In other jurisdictions, a principal or employer also has a claim against an employee who takes a bribe on the basis of loyalty owed in application of an employment contract. In practice, however, it may be difficult to prove that an act of bribery is the direct cause of a material loss.

Another kind of tort may involve taking away or harming the economic advantage of another party. This is often called "tortious interference" and is illustrated in box 4.12.

3. Unjust Enrichment

In addition to tort and contract, unjust enrichment is a separate cause of action. Its focus is on reestablishing equality between two parties when one has taken economic advantage of the other. The *raison d'être* of this theory is the injustice that lies in one

---

20. Industries & General Mortgage Co. Ltd. v. Lewis [1949] 2 All ER 573 (U.K.).

person's retaining something that he or she ought not to retain, requiring that the scales be righted.[21] There is no need to show that any loss was suffered. The elements for unjust enrichment are the receipt of a benefit and unjust retention thereof at the expense of another. The "expense of another element does not apply however when the plaintiff seeks restitution of secret profits generated by the fraud of a faithless agent. A public official is an agent and has an unqualified duty to make restitution of all secret profits."[22] Thus a state can seek restitution from corrupt officials who have taken advantage to enrich themselves.

In some jurisdictions, disgorgement of illicit profits is based on this concept of unjust enrichment. Thus some jurisdictions provide legal basis for disgorgement of illicit profits. In Germany, for example, in most cases the principal's claim for disgorgement under civil law will not create any difficulties, its basis originating directly from the contractual relationship between the principal and the agent.[23] Disgorgement does not require the principal to have suffered loss or any other disadvantage; nor does the payment have to induce the conclusion of the contract. It is sufficient that the payment of the bribe gives rise to suspicions that the agent did not exclusively serve the interest of the principal.[24]

4. Civil Actions Based on Criminal Actions

A civil claim may also arise based on the same facts as the criminal case. The evidence proving the criminal act may provide the injured party with a civil remedy, separately actionable. This commonly occurs in one of two ways. First, an act of bribery or corruption as a criminal offense may provide the basis for civil liability in a separate civil lawsuit. For example, the civil cause of action of misappropriation may have the same elements as the crime of theft or embezzlement. Second, civil actions for damages may also be part of a criminal proceeding in countries that recognize the *partie civile* (in English "civil party") to the criminal action. In considering these causes of action, one must have a solid understanding of the interplay of criminal and civil actions.

Criminal Offenses, a Basis for Civil Actions

A prior criminal conviction often makes it easier to establish the basis for civil liability. Frequently it is also possible to use evidence gathered in the course of a criminal proceeding in a civil litigation. Admissions made in the criminal case also make it easier to refute defenses put forth to counter the civil claim. Though it may seem obvious within

---

21. See Martin Kenney, "The Fundamentals of a Civil Asset Recovery Action," in *Asset Tracing and Recovery, The FraudNet World Compendium* (Berlin: Erich Schmidt Verlag, 2009).

22. See Leonard Gumport, "Public Corruption—Maximizing Remedies" (paper discussed during the County Counsels' Association of California 2005 Annual Meeting Conference, September 14–16, Los Gatos, California), http://www.grlegal.com/Articles/public_corruption_mem_7-11-06.pdf.

23. O. Meyer, "Combating Corruption by Means of Private Law: The German Experience," in *The Civil Law Consequences of Corruption* (Baden-Baden: Nomos, 2009).

24. Ibid.

More on Alamieyeseigha: *Nigeria v. Santolina Investment Corp. & Ors.* (United Kingdom and Nigeria)

The basic facts of the Alamieyeseigha cases are set out in box 1.3 above. The guilty pleas of the defendants in the criminal cases in Nigeria formed part of the legal basis that allowed Nigeria, as the plaintiff state, to obtain a summary judgment in the United Kingdom for confiscation of property and a bank account.

Nigeria brought civil proceedings in the U.K. High Court (Chancery Division) for summary judgment against two companies, Santolina Investment Corporation and Solomon and Peters Ltd., respectively incorporated in the Seychelles and the British Virgin Islands, to recover real estate properties and funds officially held by the companies. Both companies were controlled by Alamieyeseigha and used as corporate vehicles to hide assets allegedly derived from his corrupt conduct while governor of Bayelsa state. In March 2007, the U.K. judge gave a reserved judgment regarding the first application for summary judgment, as Alamieyeseigha was asserting that he had legitimate explanations for all of the assets claimed by Nigeria.

However, in July 2007, in a separate criminal proceeding in Nigeria against the aforementioned companies and the former governor, Alamieyeseigha pleaded guilty to six charges of making false declaration of assets before the Federal High Court, and also pleaded guilty on behalf of Solomon and Peters and Santolina to charges of money laundering related to bribes paid to obtain government contracts. Based on the Nigerian proceeding and other circumstantial evidence, the London High Court inferred that the bank balances and real estate investments held by the two companies controlled by Alamieyeseigha were derived from bribes, and secret profits should therefore be returned to the government of Nigeria as the legitimate owner of those assets. This change in circumstances destroyed any possibility that Alamieyeseigha would had been able to mount a reasonable defense against the suit, and accordingly the Chancery Division allowed a second hearing for summary judgment, which was granted on behalf of Nigeria.

Note: See Nigeria v. Santolina Investment Corp. & Ors. [2007] EWHC 3053 (Q.B.); and Emile van der Does de Willebois, Emily M. Halter, Robert A. Harrison, Ji Won Park, and J. C. Sharman, *The Puppet Masters: How the Corrupt Use Legal Structures to Hide Stolen Assets and What to Do about It* (Washington, DC: World Bank, 2011), 179, http://star.worldbank.org/star/publication/puppet -masters.

the same jurisdiction, an admission in a criminal case might also have influence on a judgment in a foreign jurisdiction.

When the defendant has been acquitted in criminal court, the option still remains for the victim to bring a claim for compensation before civil courts. A decision not to prosecute or a failed prosecution may also push the victims to bring a civil claim for damages against the alleged wrongdoer based on the same facts.[25] An acquittal may render a civil trial more difficult, but it will not, as a legal matter, bar a later civil claim. In common law jurisdictions, for example, the prosecutor may not be able to prove beyond a reasonable doubt that the defendant converted state property to his own use, but the plaintiff may be able to prove such a claim under a preponderance of the evidence (meaning that it was more likely than not), that the same defendant converted the property to his own use.

In civil law jurisdictions, the decision taken by a judge in a criminal case will also have an impact on the private civil lawsuits pending on the same facts, but the impact is not unlimited.

In France, for example, the principle of the "authority of a criminal judgment on a civil judgment"[26] extends to what has been "definitely, necessarily and certainly adjudicated on the facts, their qualification and the culpability."[27] Its implementation depends on the factual circumstances and on the reasons behind the judgment. For example, an acquittal before a criminal court may be justified by the nonexistence of the intentional element or of one material element of proof. In that situation, it may be possible to claim civil compensation from the defendant based, for instance, on his wrongful conduct or breach of contract. However, if the criminal judge finds out that the alleged facts were completely untrue, or that the defendant did not commit the offense, the private civil action to seek compensation for damages caused by these facts will not succeed.

In corruption cases in the United States, even if the Foreign Corrupt Practices Act (FCPA) does not provide private potential claimants with a possibility of legal redress,[28] FCPA violations may be used as a predicate for bringing civil actions under other statutes.[29] Under U.S. securities laws, for example, FCPA indictments may be a basis for civil liability.[30] An FCPA violation could also function as a predicate act to bring a civil suit under the Racketeer Influenced and Corrupt Organizations Act (RICO),[31] even though the strict requirements of civil RICO suits defeat most

---

25. For instance, and in another legal area not related to corruption, in the well-known O. J. Simpson case, the criminal prosecution against the American ex-football star did not succeed, but the civil actions brought by the victims' families did. In the civil case, the jury found Simpson liable, and he was ordered to pay $25 million in punitive damages and $8.5 million in compensatory damages; http://www.nytimes .com/1997/02/11/us/jury-decides-simpson-must-pay-25-million-in-punitive-award.html.

26. In French, "l'autorité de la chose jugée au pénal sur le civil."

27. Cour de Cassation, Civ. 2eme, 10 mai 2012, n 11-14.739.

28. See Lamb v. Phillip Morris, 915 F. 2d 1024, 1027-30 (6th Cir. 1990); J.S. Service Center Corp. and Sercenco, S.A. v. General Technical Services Co., Inc. and General Electric Company, 937 F. Supp. 216, 226-227 (S.D.N.Y. 1996).

29. See Douglas R. Young (Farella Braun & Martel LLP), "The Foreign Corrupt Practices Act as a Factor in Private Civil Litigation," http://www.fbm.com/files/Publication/2b79d8bf-740f-45c7-8ff2-9980da7c7b89 /Presentation/PublicationAttachment/e70b13d2-ecca-4bf3-807d-99b19fd76632/3C02CACD-4C60 -467B-B371-5C58427333E0_document.pdf.

30. See, for example, Glazer Capital Mgmt. LP v. Magistri, 549 F.3d 736 (9th Cir. 2008).

31. See Dooley v. United Technologies Corp., 803 F.Supp. 428 (D.D.C. 1992); and Environmental Tectonics v. W.S. Kirkpatrick, Inc., 847 F.2d 1052 (3d Cir. 1988).

attempts. Finally U.S. federal or state antitrust laws may provide the basis for civil liability against those who violate the FCPA when there is proof that the act of corruption has a negative effect on competition between companies within the United States or the state. For example, in the case of *KSC v. Lockheed Martin*, described earlier (box 4.12), the Supreme Court of California confirmed that an FCPA violation constitutes an act of unfair competition (which includes a fraudulent business act or practice) under California's unfair competition law and thus triggers liability under that law.

The Interplay of Criminal and Civil Actions

There are several elements to consider when discussing civil action based on a criminal case, including the fact that the pending criminal case may cause the judge in the civil case to suspend the private civil action until the criminal matter is concluded. In many jurisdictions, criminal proceedings are associated with the general interest of the society and lead to the most powerful sanctions against convicted persons. Thus, they may be given priority over other proceedings (civil, commercial, and administrative) based on the same facts and initiated by the same parties. This issue is of relevance for any party seeking civil remedies.

In many civil law jurisdictions, when criminal investigations and proceedings are initiated, private actions based on the same facts and seeking compensation from civil damages may be suspended until the final judgment of the criminal case. For example, in France, if a civil suit is brought to obtain compensation based on facts that are the subject of a criminal prosecution, the civil action will be suspended until the end of the criminal case. However, if the civil lawsuit concerns related but different facts or parties, or if the claim is not for compensation of damages, a suspension may be not mandatory but discretionary.[32] This legal requirement may lead to large delays in adjudicating cases, since defendants may initiate criminal proceedings when they are brought before civil courts for dilatory purposes—to postpone the results of the civil proceedings. As a result, some jurisdictions have changed their laws to allow for more flexibility. In France, criminal proceedings now only impose the suspension of civil proceedings to claim compensation for damage caused by the offense; other proceedings (for example, to declare a contract invalid) are not stayed, even if the forthcoming judgment in the criminal case might have a direct or indirect influence on their outcome.[33]

In common law jurisdictions, the criminal and civil proceedings may run in parallel. However, if a criminal action is pending and a civil suit is brought, the defendant may assert his right against self-incrimination and may be entitled to a stay of the civil lawsuit until the end of the criminal case. This is the case in the United States, unless the

---

32. Code of Criminal Procedure, Law No. 2000-516 of 15 June 2000, Article 1, Official Journal of 16 June 2000, Article 4, as modified by Law No. 2007-291 of March 5, 2007—art. 20 JORF 6 March 2007.
33. Article 4 para. 3 of the French Code of Criminal Procedure, modified by Law N° 2007-291 from March 5, 2007.

criminal action against the defendant is in another country, in which case he may not be entitled to a stay.[34]

The interplay of civil and criminal actions becomes more complicated with regard to non-parties who hold evidence important to a case. In the context of asset recovery, these may be accountants or banks. If the non-party lives in a country with a privilege against self-incrimination, and the plaintiff state is gathering evidence by using Article 11 of the Hague Convention, that non-party may try to argue on the basis of the convention that he is entitled to obtain a stay of the civil lawsuit.[35] As these matters are complex and technical, advice from competent counsel is essential to evaluate this interplay in any specific context.

Civil Action for Damages as Part of the Criminal Proceedings

The involvement of the victim—including a state or government that has been harmed by corruption offenses—in criminal proceedings is encouraged in most jurisdictions. In civil law jurisdictions, it may be possible for the victim to participate in foreign proceedings as a civil party. In most civil law jurisdictions, party status may be conferred to the victim that has suffered a direct and personal harm resulting from the criminal defendant's wrongdoing. Criminal procedures then allow the victim harmed by an offense to participate in the criminal case as a civil party and to obtain reparation if the defendant is convicted, as illustrated in box 4.14.[36]

On the one hand, this avenue is an interesting option if the jurisdiction seeking redress does not have the legal basis, capacity, or evidence to pursue an international investigation on its own. On the other hand, the jurisdiction that has been harmed by corruption offenses has no control over the proceedings, and success largely depends on the foreign authorities' priorities.[37]

In addition, there may be some limitations to the civil party status in the event that plea bargaining procedures are involved. Prosecutors may handle cases without considering the interests of the civil party, which may become a passive observer of the proceeding. Such a situation can be avoided through a proactive attitude in the legal proceedings, so as to have the prosecutor indicate to the defendant that the plea bargain will take into account the outcome of settlement discussions with the victim. Finally, some jurisdictions might also be reluctant to confer on the victim civil party status to the criminal proceedings, as potential difficulties in the calculation of damages, or the gathering of necessary evidence for the establishment of damages, might considerably prolong

---

34. See United States v. Balsys, 525 U.S. 666, 669 (1998) (non-U.S. person living in the United States, who faced civil suit in the United States, could not avoid giving testimony in the U.S. civil case by asserting that he was subject to a criminal case in another country).

35. The Hague Convention on the Taking of Evidence Abroad in Civil or Commercial Matters, 23 U.S.T. 2555, 847 U.N.T.S. 241. See chapter 6 for the full citation and explanation of how the Hague Convention can be used.

36. See chapter 1, in the section, "States and Government Entities as Civil Party in Criminal Proceedings."

37. Brun et al., *Asset Recovery Handbook*, http://star.worldbank.org/star/publication/asset-recovery-handbook.

State as Civil Party: Nigeria Awarded Damages as *Partie Civile* to Criminal Money Laundering Case against Nigerian Official (France)

Under Article 2 of the French criminal procedure code, a party may obtain civil compensation from a criminal court when the party can show personal and direct damage resulting from the crime.

In 2007, Nigeria became a *partie civile* in a money laundering case initiated against Dan Etété, former minister of energy of Nigeria. Etété was convicted and sentenced to three years' imprisonment. Nigeria, as a *partie civile*, was awarded €150,000 for nonpecuniary damages (in French, *prejudice moral*). At the same time, the court found that Nigeria had not proved a tangible pecuniary damage.

Note: Tribunal de Grand Instance (TGI) de Paris, 11eme chambre, November 7, 2007. Although Nigeria did not collect the damages because it failed to respond to appellate proceedings, the reasoning remains valid.

Illustration of Some Options of a State Party to Proceedings before Criminal and Civil Courts in a Foreign Jurisdiction

State X is trying to recover assets from its former minister of natural Resources, Mr. Y. Part of the assets are located in a foreign civil law jurisdiction, country Z.

There is a criminal case against Mr. Y in country Z. Therefore, the following options are open to state X:

- To seek civil remedies for the damage caused by the criminal offense that Mr. Y committed under a tort theory in a separate civil lawsuit. In this option, state X may have to await the final criminal judgment to pursue civil proceedings.

- To seek to intervene as a civil party in the criminal proceedings. With this option, no independent civil action is required, since civil remedies will be decided in the course of the criminal proceedings.

- To seek other legal grounds, including proprietary claims or contractual remedies. Because this civil action is not intended to obtain compensation for damages caused by the criminal offense, it may not be necessary to wait for the adjudication of the criminal offense.

Source: World Bank.

the proceedings. For example, in Germany, adhesion proceedings are extremely rare in practice (see box 4.15).[38]

---

38. See Markus Löffelmann, "The Victim in Criminal Proceedings: A Systematic Portrayal of Victim Protection under German Criminal Procedure Law," Resource Material Series No. 70, 41–68, 2006, Simon Cornell, ed., United Nations Asia and Far East Institute for the Prevention of Crime and the Treatment of Offenders (UNAFEI), http://www.unafei.or.jp/english/pdf/RS_No70/No70_06VE_Loffelmann1.pdf.

5. Civil Provisional Measures and Investigative Tools: How to Investigate and Freeze Assets

Once the state has identified possible grounds on which to bring a civil lawsuit, the plaintiff in a civil court will have to provide evidence to establish the cause of the action and secure assets, just as the prosecutor must do in a criminal action. Although the range of measures is not as wide as in criminal cases, civil procedures offer some very useful means to achieve these objectives. Whether in common or civil law systems, creative and useful tools exist to trace and secure assets wrongly acquired to ensure that they can be recovered by the plaintiff state.

A. Investigative Measures in Civil Asset Recovery Cases

Investigative tools such as disclosure and "no-say" or "gag" orders (especially in common law jurisdictions), search orders, and witness interrogations can be used to pursue a civil corruption case.

1. Early Disclosure and "No-Say" or "Gag" Orders in Common Law Countries

In common law jurisdictions, parties to existing litigation are obligated to disclose to the other side documents and other materials relevant to the claims. In some cases, the plaintiffs can also request disclosures even before formal proceedings have started.

To secure documentary evidence, a claimant may request production or disclosure of documents held by defendants (or potential defendants) and, in some cases, third parties, including banks or intermediaries. For banks, documents to be requested may include banking and financial documents, including account-opening forms, the identity of beneficial owners (of accounts, companies, and trusts), bank statements, and customer due diligence information (commonly called "know-your-customer" information).

In an example concerning the stage before formal proceedings have started, a common asset recovery scenario in the United Kingdom, Rule 31.16(3) of the Civil Procedure Rules provides the court with the discretion to make an order for disclosure where both the applicant and the respondent are likely to be parties to subsequent proceedings and disclosure is desirable so as to (a) dispose fairly of the anticipated proceedings, (b) help the dispute to be resolved without proceedings, or (c) save costs.

Norwich Pharmacal Orders: *Norwich Pharmacal Company and Others v. Customs and Excise Commissioners* (United Kingdom)

Norwich Pharmacal orders require (a) that a wrong must have been carried out, or arguably carried out, by an ultimate wrongdoer; (b) that there be a need for an order to enable an action to be brought against the ultimate wrongdoer; and (c) that the person against whom the order is sought must (a) be implicated so as to have facilitated the wrongdoing, and (b) be able, or likely to be able, to provide the information necessary to enable the ultimate wrongdoer to be sued.

Note: Norwich Pharmacal Co. v. Customs and Excise Commissioners, [1974] A.C. 133 (H.L.).

Applying these provisions to disclosure by third parties, so-called Norwich Pharmacal orders may oblige a third party involved in unlawful conduct to assist the person who suffered damage by giving them full information and disclosing the identity of wrongdoers. In the Norwich case, Norwich Pharmacal Company owned the patent for a chemical compound. Unknown persons were importing unlicensed compounds, and Norwich wanted to find out who they were and sue them. The defendants had records of who those importers were, and Norwich brought a court action to force them to disclose. The court granted the order, pronouncing that while usually only parties to litigation are obliged to disclose, the defendants had a duty to assist the party who was wronged (Norwich) by giving it any information that could disclose the identity of the wrongdoers (box 5.1).

Similarly, if an applicant demonstrates a prima facie case that his funds have been subject of a fraud or some other misappropriation, and that the funds or their proceeds have been paid by or through the bank or other entity from which disclosure is sought, a different kind of order, a "Bankers Trust" order, can be used to oblige banks to disclose relevant banking documentation.[1]

To prevent third parties from informing a defendant of a disclosure order, the court may impose a gag or no-say order, by which any breach of confidentiality may be considered contempt of court. For example, a bank may not inform its clients of specific requests toward their accounts.

2. Ex Parte *Search Orders in Common Law Jurisdictions*

Considered the "nuclear weapon of civil procedure,"[2] Anton Piller orders are search and seizure orders that require the defendant to permit the plaintiff entry to the defendant's premises so as to secure property, documents, or other material as specified in the order. The plaintiff must be able to demonstrate that if he were to file suit in the normal course, a high risk exists of loss or destruction of claimed assets.[3]

---

1. The Bankers Trust order was named as such after the decision Bankers Trust v. Shapira [1980] 1WLR 1274.
2. Bank Mellat v. Nikpour [1985] FSR 87 (CA)(U.K.).
3. J. B. Berryman, "The Anton Piller Order—A Civil Search Warrant" (paper presented at American Bar Association International Law Section Conference, Washington, DC, April 5–8, 2011), 22.

Anton Piller was a German manufacturing company specializing in generators. The company contracted with an English company called Manufacturing Process Ltd., run by two U.K. agents, to sell its machines to customers in England. Anton Piller learned that the two agents were secretly providing confidential information to German companies eager to manufacture power units like the ones that Piller made. The disclosure was supported by documents that emanated from the German competitor companies. Anton Piller asked the court for an interim injunction to restrain infringement and for an order authorizing it to enter the premises of the English company to inspect its documents and remove or copy them. The judge granted an interim injunction to stop the wrongdoing but refused to order inspection or removal of documents.

Anton Piller appealed the decision, and the Court of Appeal granted the order on the ground that the order in that case was not a search warrant: "[I]t does not authorize the plaintiffs' solicitors or anyone else to enter the Defendant's premises against his will [...]. It only authorizes entry and inspection by the permission of the Defendants [...]. It actually orders him to give permission—with, I suppose, the result that if he does not give permission, he is guilty of contempt of court."

Note: Anton Piller KG v. Manufacturing Processes Limited [1976] Ch 55.

There are three requirements: (a) there must be an extremely strong prima facie case on the merits (meaning that it looks very likely that the plaintiff will win);[4] (b) the damage, potential or actual, must be very serious for the applicant; and (c) there must be clear evidence that the defendants have incriminating documents or things in their possession and that there is a real possibility that they may destroy the material before an application *inter partes* can be made.

These Anton Piller orders are sought frequently by a plaintiff to push forward investigative measures and secure evidence, both useful tactics in asset recovery litigation (box 5.2).

Court rules in relation to interim injunctions prescribe various requirements for execution of these search orders.[5] For instance, a search order may be executed only in the presence of an independent solicitor of sufficient experience in the operation of such orders, who is not an employee or member of the applicant's firm of solicitors.[6]

To obtain an Anton Piller order, the plaintiff must submit to the court a sworn statement (an affidavit) and a Writ of Summons. The affidavit in support of the application must set forth fully the reason the order is sought, including the probability that relevant material

---

4. In legal parlance, "the merits" refers to the value and persuasiveness of the evidence in the underlying case, as opposed to the motion for temporary measures.
5. CPR Part 25 Practice Direction (Interim injunction) para. 7 (Civil Procedure Act 1997).
6. Ibid., para. 7.2, 7.6.

In 2008, Ao Man Long, former minister of transport and public works in Macao SAR, China, was convicted of corruption offenses involving about HK$800 million (approximately US$103 million). He was sentenced in Macao to 27 years' imprisonment, and a confiscation order of approximately HK$250 million (roughly US$32 million) was entered.

A significant amount of his bribery proceeds had been deposited into accounts in Hong Kong SAR, China. There was no mutual legal assistance (MLA) agreement between the jurisdictions, but authorities in Macao SAR, China, used informal channels (the Hong Kong Independent Commission against Corruption) to restrain the proceeds and obtain search warrants. Because MLA channels were unavailable to recover the proceeds, Macao SAR, China, subsequently launched a civil suit in Hong Kong SAR, China, for more than HK$230 million (approximately US$30 million). The original restraint order, obtained pursuant to antibribery legislation in Hong Kong SAR, China, remained in place even though a criminal prosecution was not launched in that jurisdiction.

Source: Simon N. M. Young, "Why Civil Actions against Corruption?" *Journal of Financial Crime* 16, no. 2 (2009): 144–59.

would disappear if the order were not made, as well as provide a detailed description of the premises where the evidence is located and the experience of the independent solicitor.[7]

It is important to note that since the application for a search order is inevitably made without notice (referred to in legal parlance as *ex parte*) to the respondent, in such circumstances the supporting affidavit must be made on a "full and frank" basis. That means that the applicant should not only disclose facts that support its application but also refer to arguments, within its knowledge, that the respondent may have advanced to rebut the application, had the respondent been given an opportunity to do so at the application hearing. The same principle applies to applications for freezing injunctions made on an *ex parte* basis (box 5.3).

3. Early Disclosure and Search Orders in Civil Law Jurisdictions

Requesting pretrial disclosures and search orders is also possible in some civil law jurisdictions.[8] Parties may be allowed to ask a judge, *ex parte*, to take legally admissible investigative measures if there is a legitimate reason to conserve or establish, before any trial, evidence of facts on which the resolution of a case could depend. For example, Articles 139 and 145 of the French *Code de Procedure Civile* allow the judge to take investigative steps to collect information useful for future proceedings. This action, known as *instruction in futurum*, is commonly used in France in proceedings concerning tort, proprietary claims, or breach of contract.

---

7. Ibid., para. 7.3.
8. This is not the case in Germany.

4. Evidence from Witnesses

A witness is someone who, either voluntarily or under compulsion, provides testimonial evidence, either oral or written, of what he or she knows, or claims to know, about the matter before a court or an authorized official. Evidence provided by witnesses, including expert witnesses, is frequently very important in asset recovery cases in both criminal and civil proceedings.

In many jurisdictions, parties to civil litigation may request that witnesses provide testimony in court, before a delegate judge, before a deposition officer, or simply before the requesting attorney.[9] The testimony may be provided in public or in a confidential setting. As described later in the book, in the discussion on using insolvency as a tool for recovery, defendants themselves may be compelled under insolvency laws to testify as to the location of assets.[10]

Defendants in asset recovery cases are often ordered or required at an early stage in the proceedings to provide a witness statement disclosing how they acquired assets or a statement of all their assets. It is often difficult for a corrupt defendant to produce a plausible statement or one that is unlikely to ultimately incriminate him. This can be a very effective pressure point on the defendant. An example of such a situation appears in box 5.4.

BOX 5.4	A Defendant Fails to Disclose Assets: *JSC BTA Bank v. Ablyazov & Others* (United Kingdom)

In the United Kingdom, a bank headquartered in Kazakhstan sued its former chairman, Mr. Ablyazov, for misappropriation of the assets of the bank. The bank sought a freeze of the assets. At an early stage in the proceedings, in conjunction with the freeze order, Ablyazov was required to provide full disclosure of his assets.

Ablyazov appealed the order, claiming his privilege against self-incrimination, in particular that compliance with the order might lead him to disclose information that could be used against him in criminal proceedings in Kazakhstan. His appeal was dismissed for a variety of reasons, although the bank agreed that the disclosure be initially confined to the claimants' solicitors and counsel, with the issue of wider disclosure to be resolved at a later date. Eventually, Ablyazov was found guilty in absentia for failing to disclose his assets and lying under oath in an affidavit and sentenced to 16 to 22 months in prison.

Note: JSC BTA Bank v. Ablyazov & Others [2009] EWCA (iv) 1125; see also box 9.2, in chapter 9, "Use of a Receiver to Preserve Assets."

---

9. For example, in the United States in civil litigation it is very common for the attorneys to give notice and compel the presence of a witness to give sworn testimony before a court reporter and opposing counsel, without the need for the presence of a judge.

10. There has been some attempt on the part of such defendants to try to use the "right against self-incrimination" where it exists, but in the U.K., the *Maxwell* case ruled against that defense, and so targets, that is, the debtors in an insolvency proceeding, can be compelled to testify under penalty of imprisonment for refusing. Bishopsgate Investment Management Ltd. v. Maxwell (No. 2) [1993] BCLC 814; see also chapter 9.

5. Third Party Disclosure Orders

As noted above, under English civil procedure rules, the court can compel third parties to disclose documents even before formal proceedings have started, if such disclosure is likely to support the case of the applicant and if the disclosure is necessary to permit the claim to be determined fairly and to save costs.[11] Third party disclosure orders are also used after formal proceedings are initiated against banks in grand corruption cases. The illustration in box 5.5 shows that they can also be used in more unusual circumstances.

Practitioners must take into account that transaction methods have changed tremendously over the last decade. Electronic communication and transactions have come to

---

BOX 5.5	An Example of a Third Party Disclosure Order: More on the Case of *Nigeria v. Santolina Investment Corp., Diepreye Alamieyeseigha & Others* (United Kingdom)

The basic facts of this case are set out in box 1.3, in chapter 1.

During his time in office, Diepreye Alamieyeseigha accumulated a portfolio of foreign assets, including four London properties acquired for a total of £4.6 million, a Cape Town penthouse, and £1 million in cash stored at one of his London properties. The bulk of his foreign assets were held in offshore companies and trusts. In September 2005, Alamieyeseigha was arrested by the U.K. police on three counts of money laundering. He was granted bail but managed to flee the jurisdiction, allegedly by disguising himself as a woman.

Some of Alamieyeseigha's assets were recovered by the U.K. authorities using criminal and civil mechanisms, but his properties and bank balances remained untouched. Nigeria therefore brought civil proceedings in the United Kingdom to recover the bank balances and properties. The Metropolitan Police had obtained a wealth of evidence of Alamieyeseigha's corrupt activities in Nigeria and the laundering of the proceeds internationally. To move its proceedings forward, Nigeria needed that U.K. evidence. However, the evidence had been obtained by the Metropolitan Police using its compulsory powers; the police owed duties of confidence to the owners of the documents, which prevented them from voluntarily providing the documents to Nigeria and its lawyers for use in the civil proceedings.

In this case, Nigeria applied (without notice to Alamieyeseigha) for an order requiring the Metropolitan Police to disclose the evidence it had collected. Nigeria argued that it was in the public interest to do so. The Metropolitan Police confirmed that it did not oppose the application, and, most important, that the disclosure would not jeopardize further criminal investigations.

Note: See London High Court of Justice, November 25, 2005, Case No.: CO/9133/2005; and Nigeria v. Santolina Investment Corp. & Ors., [2007] EWHC 3053 (Q.B.).

---

11. Rule 31.17 of the Civil Procedure Rules, United Kingdom, available at http://www.justice.gov.uk/courts /procedure-rules/civil/rules/part31.

dominate the economic landscape. In fact, some experts have estimated that 93 percent of corporate documents are created, viewed, and stored electronically,[12] and that 70 percent of those documents never migrate to paper.[13] Therefore, when examining "books and records" of any company or individual, it is important that electronic communications and transactional evidence be examined as well. Beyond copies of electronic communications is a history attached to each communication, such as authors and past authors, hidden text, distribution lists, dates, and so forth, which together are called "metadata." The metadata are often crucial in tracing assets. Specialist individuals and firms can uncover the metadata that often constitute the trail to assets to be recovered.

B. Securing the Assets: Provisional Measures in Civil Proceedings

Restraint, freezing, or seizure orders are frequently used to restrain assets suspected of being the proceeds of a crime. Seizure involves taking physical possession of the targeted asset, whereas restraint may involve securing or freezing without taking possession. Court orders are generally required, but some law enforcement agencies in certain jurisdictions are granted a limited right to seize assets, at least provisionally. Restraint orders are a form of mandatory injunction issued by a judge or a court that restrains any person from dealing with or disposing of the assets named in the order, pending the determination of confiscation proceedings (table 5.1).

1. Freezing and Restraining Orders

In a number of common law jurisdictions, worldwide freezing orders commonly called "Mareva injunctions" may be used. Various provisional measures may also be available.

TABLE 5.1	Types of Orders for Provisional Measure	
	Seizure order	Restraint order
Definition	Physical possession of the targeted assets.	Restraining any person from dealing with or disposing of the assets named in the order.
Authority granting the order	Court authorization generally required, but some jurisdictions grant law enforcement agencies or prosecutors some right to seize assets.	Court authorization generally required, but some jurisdictions permit restraint to be ordered by prosecutors or other law enforcement authorities.
Examples of order	Provisional seizure (*saisie conservatoire*, France).	Mareva injunction (common law).
Source: World Bank.		

---

12. Kevin Craine, *Designing a Document Strategy* (Hurst, TX: McGrew & McDaniel Group, 2000), www.mcgrewmcdaniel.com; cited in a presentation by a prominent U.K. asset recovery specialist.
13. Dana Hawkins, "Office Politics in the Electronic Age," *U.S. News & World Report Online*, February 2000; cited in a presentation by a prominent U.K. asset recovery specialist.

Mareva Injunctions

In British Commonwealth law jurisdictions, freezing orders are derived from the so-called Mareva injunction, issued in the case *Mareva Compania Naviera S.A. v. International Bulkcarriers S.A.* (1975) and enacted in Section 37 of the U.K. Supreme Court Act 1981. These orders may be granted to prevent defendants from removing assets from the jurisdiction or otherwise dealing with the assets. To obtain a Mareva injunction, a claimant needs to provide

- An arguable case on the merits;
- A real risk of unjustifiable dissipation of assets; and
- Assurance that the order is just and convenient in all the circumstances.

The Civil Procedure Rules of the United Kingdom provide that the injunction may be granted in relation to assets "whether located within the jurisdiction or not" (CPR 25.1(1) (f)).

Keep in mind that freezing orders do not imply any transfer of property between the claimant and the defendant, and that further proof will be required to obtain a seizure order (box 5.6).

Provisional Measures Available in Civil Law Jurisdictions: The French Example

In civil law jurisdictions as well, legal tools to seize or freeze assets are available. In France, for example, the *Code des Procedures Civiles d'Execution* (CPCEx) addresses potential civil remedies in asset recovery cases. In particular, article L.111-1[14] provides that any creditor is entitled to a provisional measure to ensure that his rights are respected. Similarly, Article L.511-1 of CPCEx provides for temporary seizure of assets: A claimant may request, ex parte, to be granted a freezing order on assets belonging to the defendant if the credit presently exists (*fondée en son principe*) and is believed to be in danger of dissipation (*circonstances susceptibles de menacer le recouvrement de la créance*). The procedure is very informal, and the claimant has to bring a request to a specific judge (*juge de l'exécution*).

This special judge can grant a provisional order to seize the assets. However, the French law distinguishes between seizures that apply to most personal property (tangible or intangible, including bank accounts and debts) and judicial security measures that apply mostly to real property. Plus, to be effective, judicial security measures on real property must be registered with the Land Registry.[15]

This type of seizure is of great interest for creditors who seek to secure assets that are believed to be held in financial institutions. By asking the judge to order a provisional

---

14. Art. L. 111-1 CPCEx reads as follows: "*Tout créancier peut pratiquer une mesure conservatoire pour assurer la sauvegarde de ses droits.*"
15. Bernd H. Klose, ed., *Asset Tracing and Recovery—The FraudNet World Compendium* (Berlin: Erich Schmidt Verlag GmbH & Co., 2009), 116.

Mareva Injunctions and Worldwide Freezing Order

Mareva Compania Naviera S.A. (the plaintiffs) owned the vessel *Mareva*. They leased it to International Bulkcarriers S.A. (the defendants), the charterers, on a time charter for a trip out to East Asia and back. The charterers subchartered the vessel. The charterers received payment on a London-based bank account from the subcontractor but did not pay back the plaintiffs the full amount due. Therefore, the plaintiffs claimed the unpaid hire and damages for the repudiation. Among other procedures, they applied for an injunction to prevent the defendants from disposing of the money in the London bank, arguing that there was a grave danger that the money in the bank in London would disappear. A court granted a limited-time restraining injunction on the basis of an ex parte application but then refused to extend it. On appeal, the Court of Appeal then granted the extended injunction, which became known as a "Mareva" injunction.

Sentencing by Lord Denning summarized the legal concept of the Mareva injunction:

> If it appears that the debt is due and owing, and there is a danger that the debtor may dispose of his assets so as to defeat it before judgment, the court has jurisdiction in a proper case to grant an interlocutory judgment so as to prevent him disposing of those assets. It seems to me that this is a proper case for the exercise of this jurisdiction. There is money in a bank in London which stands in the name of these charterers. The charterers have control of it. They may at any time dispose of it or remove it out of this country. If they do so, the ship-owners may never get their charter hire. The ship is now on the high seas. It has passed Cape Town on its way to India. It will complete the voyage and the cargo will be discharged. And the ship-owners may not get their charter hire at all. In face of this danger, I think this court ought to grant an injunction to restrain the charterers from disposing of these moneys now in the bank in London until the trial or judgment in this action. If the charterers have any grievance about it when they hear of it, they can apply to discharge it. But meanwhile the ship-owners should be protected. It is only just and right that this court should grant an injunction. I would therefore continue the injunction.

Source: Mareva Compania Naviera SA v. International Bulkcarriers SA, [1980] 1 All ER 213.

seizure of assets belonging to the debtor, the creditor or plaintiff state may obtain an order to force financial institutions to freeze (or "block") the assets.

2. Other Tools to Secure Assets

Other tools to secure assets include "Mareva by letter," proprietary injunctions, and appointment of a provisional administrator, receiver, or liquidator.

"Mareva by Letter"
In a case where proceeds of corruption are deposited in a bank account, the "Mareva by letter" constitutes another opportunity to protect and preserve the targeted assets. The Mareva by letter is a notice to a third party guardian or holder of assets, such as a bank, informing them that those assets may be subject to a constructive trust. In other words,

it informs the holder of the assets that the person it has on record as the true owner may, as a legal matter, hold those assets in constructive trust for someone else.[16] The Mareva by letter leads to the freezing of such assets if the three conditions listed above are fulfilled (arguable case on merits, real risk of dissipation, and justness of the order). By placing a bank on notice that it is being used for fraudulent activity, leaving it vulnerable to possible private and public law action if it does not prevent the further misuse of funds, a bank may of its own volition take steps to prevent the funds' being released.

The procedure is relatively simple: A freeze may be effected by issuing a letter to the asset holder or guardian in question, informing them of the true origin or beneficial ownership of the targeted funds or assets, and advising them of their potential accessory civil and possible criminal liability in the event of any transfer or disposal of the assets in question. This procedure should, however, be accompanied by other actions, either criminal or civil. For example, the party seeking to recover stolen assets may obtain proprietary injunctions or the appointment of a provisional administrator or liquidator. The danger in not taking some form of injunctive relief at the same time as sending the letter is that the Mareva by letter may put the defendant on notice that a victim party is trying to recover its assets, and if the bank does not agree to take steps to prevent the movement of the funds in question, the defendant may transfer the money out of the reach of the victim.

Proprietary Injunctions

A proprietary injunction concerns the property or the traceable proceeds of the property (the so-called proprietary assets) of the defendant and prohibits dealing in that asset. The claimant has to show an arguable case and that it is just and convenient to grant the order. There is no need to prove a risk of dissipation, since the defendant is holding the claimant's assets.

The Appointment of a Provisional Administrator, Receiver, or Liquidator

In the case of failing corporate entities, the appointment of a provisional administrator, receiver, or liquidator is a pragmatic method to secure and trace assets placed in a company and its subsidiaries. One of the missions of the receiver, in particular, will be to ascertain that assets targeted by the measures will be collected and preserved, so that plaintiffs can recover their assets.

---

16. Martin S. Kenney, "Mareva by Letter—Preserving Assets Extra-Judicially, Destroying a Bank's Defense of Good Faith by Exposing It to Actual Knowledge of Fraud (paper prepared for the ICC FraudNet Conference, London, September 21, 2006).

6. Legal Tools for International Cooperation: How to Obtain the Supporting Evidence

In transnational civil cases, practitioners must bear in mind that international cooperation is essential for the successful recovery of assets that are hidden in foreign jurisdictions. In particular, cooperation is needed to gather evidence, to implement provisional measures, to enforce judgments, and eventually to confiscate the proceeds of corruption. In criminal matters, international cooperation generally includes "informal assistance" and more formal mutual legal assistance (MLA) requests.[1]

Although they are less forceful, similar avenues exist in civil law. To file a request for assistance in international civil matters, a legal ground (a "basis") must exist in the law to permit or compel the assistance requested. That basis must be specified in the request. The legal ground may come through (a) multilateral conventions (such as the UN Convention Against Corruption), treaties, or agreements containing provisions on requests for assistance in international in civil matters; (b) bilateral mutual assistance treaties and agreements, (c) domestic legislation allowing for international cooperation in civil cases, or (d) a promise of reciprocity through diplomatic channels, referred to as "letters rogatory" or "comity" in some jurisdictions.[2]

A. International Conventions Promoting International Cooperation

Although international judicial assistance is possible without formal international agreements, the existence of such agreements generally improves cooperation among national courts.[3] Indeed, some multilateral conventions, treaties, and agreements contain provisions that oblige or encourage signatories to provide mutual legal assistance under international law.

---

1. Jean-Pierre Brun, Clive Scott, Kevin M. Stephenson, and Larissa Gray, *Asset Recovery Handbook: A Guide for Practitioners* (Washington, DC: World Bank, 2011), 6, http://star.worldbank.org/star/publication/asset -recovery-handbook. The third branch, extradition, only applies in criminal cases.
2. Ibid., 138–39.
3. Gary Born, *International Civil Litigation in United States Courts: Commentary and Materials*, Kluwer Law International; 3d ed. (1997).

1. The UN Convention Against Corruption (UNCAC)

The United Nations Convention Against Corruption, or UNCAC, is the most widely applicable international treaty addressing international cooperation in the context of corruption. It has been signed by 171 countries and obliges states parties to afford one another the widest measures of assistance in investigations, prosecutions, and judicial proceedings concerning corruption matters.[4] UNCAC specifically addresses recovery of proceeds of corruption.

In particular, UNCAC Article 43 provides, "States Parties *shall* cooperate in criminal matters in accordance with Articles 44 to 50 of the Convention. Where appropriate and consistent with their domestic legal system, States Parties *shall consider* assisting each other in investigations of and proceedings in civil and administrative matters relating to corruption" (emphasis added). Although this formulation seems to exclude mandatory application in civil matters, it still provides strong encouragement for voluntary assistance. Thus, parties may use Article 43 as a legal basis for accepting and facilitating mutual legal assistance in civil matters. Pursuant to Article 46 of UNCAC, paragraph 8, states parties cannot decline to render mutual legal assistance pursuant to Article 46 for bank secrecy reasons.

2. The Hague Conventions

The Hague Conventions on Civil Procedure and on the Taking of Evidence Abroad are designed to facilitate the transmission and execution of letters of request, further the accommodation of the different methods of evidence exchange, and improve mutual judicial cooperation in civil and commercial matters. The conventions provide for minimum standards for international judicial cooperation by simplifying the various procedures followed to take evidence abroad.[5] These conventions deal with letters of request, as well as the taking of evidence by diplomatic officers, consular agents, and commissioners.[6]

"Letters of request" are the main vehicle by which a judicial authority of a contracting state requests, from the competent authority of another contracting state, evidence or the performance of some judicial act. Thus, the attorney for the plaintiff first submits a request to the appropriate judicial authority of his own state, who then prepares a request to the state from which the evidence is requested.

Under Article 2, a "central authority" is designated to receive letters of request from judicial authorities of other contracting states and to transmit them to the authority

---

4. Ibid., 139.

5. See Robert J. Augustine, "Obtaining International Judicial Assistance under the Federal Rules and the Hague Convention on the Taking of Evidence Abroad in Civil and Commercial Matters: An Exposition of the Procedures and a Practical Example: In re Westinghouse Uranium Contract Litigation," *Georgia Journal of International Law & Comparative Law* 10, no. 1 (1980), 101.

6. See Council of Europe, "International Judicial Cooperation in Civil Matters: Taking of Evidence in Civil and Commercial Matters," http://www.coe.int/t/dghl/cooperation/lisbonnetwork/themis/Civil/Paper4_en.asp#P153_10008.

competent to execute them. The applicable law is the law of the judicial authority that executes the letter of request (in other words, the receiving state). The requested authority shall apply the appropriate measures of compulsion, as are provided by its internal law, for the execution of orders issued by the authorities of its own country.

A requested state can refuse to execute a letter of request only if the execution of the letter does not fall within the functions of the judiciary in the requested state, or if the requested state considers that its sovereignty or security would be prejudiced thereby (Article 12).

Carrying out what is requested in a letter shall not give rise to any reimbursement of taxes or costs of any nature. However, the state of execution has the right to require the state of origin to reimburse fees paid to experts and interpreters and the costs occasioned by the use of a special procedure that is requested.

The diagram in figure 6.1 describes how to obtain evidence abroad in civil or commercial matters under the Hague Convention.

In practice, the convention is frequently used to secure oral evidence from a witness and to obtain bank records, responses to interrogatories, inspection of real and

FIGURE 6.1 How to Obtain Evidence Abroad in Civil or Commercial Matters

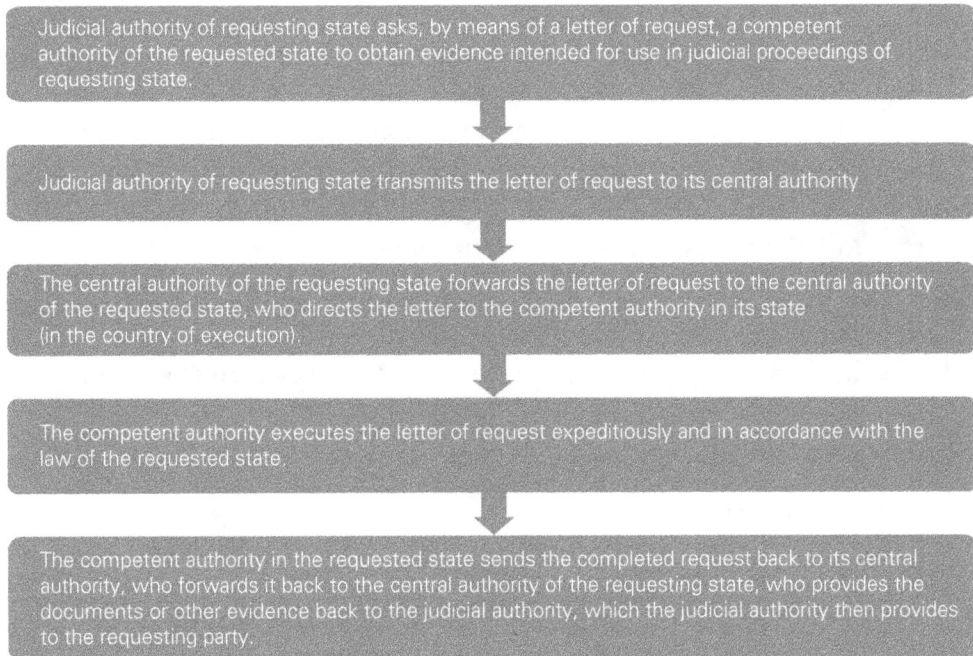

Judicial authority of requesting state asks, by means of a letter of request, a competent authority of the requested state to obtain evidence intended for use in judicial proceedings of requesting state.

↓

Judicial authority of requesting state transmits the letter of request to its central authority

↓

The central authority of the requesting state forwards the letter of request to the central authority of the requested state, who directs the letter to the competent authority in its state (in the country of execution).

↓

The competent authority executes the letter of request expeditiously and in accordance with the law of the requested state.

↓

The competent authority in the requested state sends the completed request back to its central authority, who forwards it back to the central authority of the requesting state, who provides the documents or other evidence back to the judicial authority, which the judicial authority then provides to the requesting party.

Source: World Bank.

BOX 6.1	Using the Hague Conventions to Request Banking Documentation

Australia: *Sykes v. Richardson* (2007) NSWSC 418.

The Supreme Court of New South Wales considered a letter of request relating to antitrust proceedings in the United States. The court rejected the contention that such proceedings were not "civil or commercial" in nature, despite the possibility that punitive damages might be awarded and granted assistance.

Hong Kong SAR, China: *Prediwave Corporation v. New World TMT Limited* and *Modern Office Technology Ltd. v. New World TMT Ltd.* (2006) HKCA 392; CACV000292/2006, 17 October 2006.

These cases involved a letter of request from the United States seeking the disclosure of certain categories of banking documents and were challenged on the basis (among others) that banking secrecy should prevent the disclosure of the documents. The Hong Kong SAR, China, Court of Appeal argued that banking confidentiality is not sufficient to outweigh the public interest of assisting the foreign court.

Source: World Bank.

personal property, and information concerning a person's income. Responses to requests are generally returned in a time frame of six months to one year (see box 6.1).[7]

The Convention on the Service Abroad of Judicial and Extrajudicial Documents in Civil or Commercial Matters,[8] known as the Hague Service Convention, improves mutual judicial assistance as well, by creating appropriate means to ensure that judicial and extrajudicial documents can be served abroad in sufficient time.[9] It allows service of process of court documents within signatory states without the use of consular and diplomatic channels.

3. Other Relevant Conventions or Instruments

Other conventions, including the OECD Convention on Combating Bribery of Foreign Public Officials in International Business Transactions, may be relevant for international judicial or legal assistance. Article 9 § 1 of the OECD Convention calls for international cooperation not only for the purpose of criminal investigations and proceedings but

---

7. There were 1,500 uses of chapter 1, and 2,500 uses of chapter 2, in 2007, according to responses to a questionnaire sent in 2008 to parties.

8. Convention concluded on November 15, 1965, available at http://www.hcch.net/index_en.php?act=conventions.text&cid=17.

9. "Service of process" is the procedure by which a party to a lawsuit gives an appropriate notice of initial legal action to the defendant, so as to enable that person to respond to the proceeding before the court or other tribunal. Notice is furnished by delivering a set of judicial documents ("process") to the person to be served. Service of process enables the court to assert its jurisdiction over the parties and the controversy.

also for noncriminal proceedings within the scope of the convention.[10] Practitioners may consider these conventions in specific cases to conduct or facilitate international cooperation processes.

B. Regional Instruments to Facilitate Mutual Legal Assistance

Certain regional treaties are also helpful. Within the European Union, Council Regulation 1206/2001, of May 28, 2001, Cooperation between the Courts of the Member States in the Taking of Evidence in Civil or Commercial Matters, provides two options for taking evidence in another member state. The first one concerns the direct transmission between courts, and the second concerns the direct taking of evidence by the requesting court. In the first case, the court of a member state requests the competent court of another to take evidence that is needed in judicial proceedings. In the second case, the judge of a member state can ask the judge of another member state to collect the evidence in that state, either directly or through other designated persons.

Direct taking of evidence may only take place if it can be done on a voluntary basis, without the need for coercive measures. It is performed by a member of the judiciary or by any other person, such as an expert, in accordance with the law of the member state of the requesting court. Under Article 3, a central body is designated by each member state to supply information to the courts, seek solutions to difficulties, and forward a request to the competent court in exceptional cases, when asked to do so by a requesting court. According to the regulation, requests should be executed without delay—at the latest, within 90 days of receipt—and in accordance with the law of the requested state (Article 10). The requested court shall, without delay, send to the requesting court the documents establishing the execution of the request (Article 16).

Similarly for the Americas, the Inter-American Convention on the Taking Evidence Abroad, of 1975, also addresses the topic. According to the Additional Protocol to the Inter-American Convention on the Taking of Evidence Abroad, of 1984, the central authority of a state party sends the letter rogatory to the central authority of another state party. The latter transmits the letter rogatory to the appropriate judicial or other adjudicatory authority for processing (Article 3).

---

10. OECD Convention on Combating Bribery of Foreign Public Officials in International Business Transactions, Article 9 paragraph 1: "Each Party shall, to the fullest extent possible under its laws and relevant treaties and arrangements, provide prompt and effective legal assistance to another Party for the purpose of criminal investigations and proceedings brought by a Party concerning offences within the scope of this Convention and for non-criminal proceedings within the scope of this Convention brought by a Party against a legal person. The requested Party shall inform the requesting Party, without delay, of any additional information or documents needed to support the request for assistance and, where requested, of the status and outcome of the request for assistance." Text available at http://www.oecd.org /daf/anti-bribery/ConvCombatBribery_ENG.pdf.

C. Factors to Consider When Collecting Evidence in Foreign Jurisdictions

1. Potential Legal Obstacles to Collecting Evidence in Foreign Jurisdictions: The Blocking Statutes

Practitioners should be aware that directly collecting evidence in foreign jurisdictions may not always be possible or efficient. Some countries have "blocking statutes" that restrict or prohibit the transfer of documents and other data for use in foreign proceedings, unless the transfer complies with the Hague Evidence Convention (see box 6.2).

2. Considerations When Requesting Mutual Legal Assistance in Civil Matters under International Instruments

When states and their counsel consider requesting mutual legal assistance in the context of civil matters, they should consider the following relevant factors, which are important when seeking international cooperation:

- Whether a bilateral agreement or multilateral treaty exists in which states concerned are signatories and which governs international cooperation in the context of civil litigation
- Whether the matter is purely civil or has a criminal component
- The legal system of the country from which cooperation is sought
- Whether "blocking" legislation or data protection laws exist (see below)
- Whether the country from which cooperation is sought has any particular restrictions or prohibitions with regard to the service of process, taking of evidence, or recognition and enforcement of judgments
- The procedural safeguards for the parties concerned

BOX 6.2   Blocking Statutes: The Example of France

The French blocking statute attaches criminal penalties to exporting information for use in foreign legal proceedings unless within the framework of the Hague conventions. Specifically, Article 1 *bis* prohibits "any individual to request, to investigate, or to communicate in writing, orally or by any other means, documents or information relating to economic, commercial, industrial, financial, or technical matters leading to the establishment of proof with a view to foreign administrative or judicial proceedings or as part of such proceedings." Article 1 *bis* applies "subject to treaties or international agreements and laws and regulations." Thus, exporting certain categories of documents, or responding to discovery requests relating to the economic, commercial, or financial matters is forbidden. The only acceptable means of exchanging information is through the Hague Evidence Convention or through requests for international mutual legal assistance in civil matters.

Note: French Act No. 68-678 dated July 26, 1968, relating to the communication of economic, commercial, industrial, financial, or technical documents and information to foreign natural and legal persons, as modified by French Act No. 80-538 dated July 16, 1980.

In particular, international cooperation on asset recovery through civil remedies might be hindered on the receiving side by insufficient laws and procedures and limited resources with which to provide assistance. Some countries might also have in place laws that impose limitations on their participation in judicial assistance proceedings for the taking of evidence, including laws on the protection of sovereignty, bank secrecy, trade secrets, confidentiality, and protection of sources.

In addition to the blocking statutes discussed above, two other important types of laws may affect the ability to secure evidence or assets from abroad during civil litigation: laws protecting personal data and laws imposing disclosure obligations. Boxes 6.3 and 6.4 illustrate each.

BOX 6.3   Personal Data Protection Laws within the European Union

At the European level, examples include the following:

- Directive 95/46/EC of the European Parliament and of the Council, of October 24, 1995, on the protection of individuals with regard to the processing of personal data and on the free movement of such data.

- Directive 2002/58/EC, concerning the processing of personal data and the protection of privacy in the electronic communications sector (Directive on Privacy and Electronic Communications).

- Each EU country implements the directive in its own way, creating a complex system of privacy legislation that may limit information that can be obtained through civil discovery for lawsuits.

Source: World Bank.

BOX 6.4   Disclosure Obligations in Luxembourg and Switzerland

Specific disclosure laws in Luxembourg and Switzerland require notification to the asset holder of the execution of an MLA request in civil cases, in order to provide the person an opportunity to contest the provision of the requested assistance. This notice alerts him that an investigation is being carried out and gives him the opportunity to hide or dissipate his assets and delay or block the entire process. It has thus been suggested that to fight corruption effectively, such advance notices should be lifted, especially in cases where the risk of dissipation is high.

Note: OECD (Organisation for International Co-operation and Development), *Tracking Anti-Corruption and Asset Recovery Commitments* (Washington, DC: OECD and IBRD/World Bank, 2011), 39; see also Kevin Stephenson, Larissa Gray, and Ric Power, *Barriers to Asset Recovery: An Analysis of the Key Barriers and Recommendations for Action* (Washington, DC: World Bank, 2011), 56–57 (StAR Initiative).

Practitioners should consider whether these conventions may or must be used in specific cases to conduct or facilitate international cooperation processes. Beyond these international legal tools, practitioners should keep in mind the importance of informal assistance and the role of quiet diplomacy in civil recovery cases. Moreover, the recovery of stolen assets can sometimes be facilitated by states or international organizations.

7. Damages and Compensation: How Much to Sue For?

When filing a civil lawsuit to recover assets, it is important at the outset to estimate the amount of possible recovery. The issues of quantification of the proceeds and the financial consequences of corrupt activities thus naturally arise. This chapter discusses various methods of calculating what authorities might expect to recover—the value of stolen assets or the amounts of damages to be sought in a civil lawsuit. Some methods of calculation overlap with ones used in similar criminal or other enforcement matters.

Although it is far from an exact science, some calculations can be made, and theories must be explored at the outset of any litigation. The approach taken to quantify the benefits or the damages generated by corruption depends on the type of legal action and the corresponding remedy in each particular case.[1] Often there is no clear guidance from courts on which methods to use in civil actions involving corruption. As in deciding what claim to bring, calculating the amount to be recovered will be a matter to be discussed with competent counsel in the particular jurisdiction where the legal action has been brought or is contemplated. Nonetheless, it is helpful to have a conceptual overview of the theories under consideration by various courts and scholars.

Finally, making parties "whole," or even taking away their profit, does not guarantee a deterrent punishment. That is the reason why other civil remedies, including punitive damages and the calculation of a "social damage," are sometimes invoked to achieve such a goal. Whether deterrence is properly a matter for civil law remains a question of debate, however. The final section of this chapter discusses emerging theories that could be considered or tested to address these issues (B).

A. Methods Used to Quantify Compensation, Restitution, or Illicit Proceeds

Different approaches may be considered to determine the amount to claim from private civil actions, depending on the legal basis for the action or the remedies used. The methods are related to compensation, contractual restitution, and disgorgement of illegal proceeds. All three categories may also exist in a single case.

---

1. See analytically for all remedies, A joint OECD/StAR analysis, OECD/World Bank, *Identification and Quantification of the Proceeds of Bribery*, rev. ed., p. 29, February 2012, OECD Publishing, http://dx.doi .org/10.1787/9789264174801-en.

1. Compensation for Damages

Where a state is an identifiable victim of corruption, the state may seek compensatory damages in civil courts. Compensatory damages provide plaintiffs with the strict monetary amount necessary to recover from actual injury or economic loss as a result of corrupt acts. The basic rule in determining compensatory damages is that the victim must be placed as much as possible in the circumstances in which he or she would have been but for the bribe or corrupt conduct. In government contracts, compensation may be based on tort claims when the damage results from corruption during the negotiation stage. If corruption occurred during the contract execution, contractual damages may be awarded. In this case, the contract itself may provide for liquidated damages, as illustrated in box 7.1.[2]

Courts may have to estimate, for example, the difference between the price or the quality of goods and services provided by the briber, and the price or quality to which the customer was entitled, if its agent had not taken the bribe.[3]

The goal is to set a level of damages that puts the state in the position it would have been in absent the corruption. In that context, several factors should be taken into account. First, the company's profits will be an insufficient measure of the damages in such cases. More broadly, the profit gained by the contractor will often equal the harm suffered by the state only if the effect of the corruption was to shift some of the net monetary gains of a given project from the state to the company. However, if the type of project itself, its size, or the way it was performed is affected by bribes as well, then the loss suffered may be larger.[4] The damages accordingly should be closer to the entire cost of the project, to make the state as close to whole as possible. In addition, the harm to the state may exceed the profit of the bribe payer if one takes into account the state's transaction costs, or if courts calculate "moral" or "reputational" damages (box 7.2).

2. Restitution Based on Voiding Contracts

In corruption cases, the main contract between the state and the briber may be considered invalid, as discussed earlier. Contracting states may apply to the court to declare the tainted contract null and void, in addition to their right to claim for damages.

If the court agrees and invalidates the contract, the state may be entitled to recover all sums paid pursuant to the contract (the gross revenue), or revenues after the deduction of the value of expenses and performance incurred by the briber (the net revenue).[5] In some jurisdictions courts have held that the state was entitled to recover

---

2. "Liquidated damages" means that the parties decide when they enter into the contract how much would be paid in the event of a breach of the contract.
3. OECD/World Bank, *Identification and Quantification of the Proceeds of Bribery*, rev. ed., 33.
4. A few examples: a dam is built that has few overall benefits; a road is built where there is little traffic; a power plant is excessively large; or the military buys equipment that is not needed.
5. OECD/World Bank, *Identification and Quantification of the Proceeds of Bribery*, rev. ed., 36.

The claimant, Fyffes Group, was involved in the banana trade and needed shipping services. Over a four-year period, an employee of Fyffes indirectly took bribes amounting to over US$1.4 million from a shipping company, in exchange for negotiating contracts between Fyffes and the shipping company that were favorable to the shipping company.

Fyffes sought to recover damages from the employee, the bribe-paying shipping company, and its agents.[a] According to the court, there was no dispute that the bribes had influenced the shipping company in calculating the amount of freight for each year. As a result, all defendants were found jointly liable for the value of the bribes.

In addition, the shipping company and its agent (the briber) were liable to pay additional compensation for the loss that Fyffes had undergone from entering into the contracts under unfavorable terms. To calculate this liability, the court found, first, that Fyffes would have entered into a service agreement with the shipping company even if the employee had not been dishonest. As a result, "ordinary" profits, resulting from the application of quantity or rates of shipment that would have normally been earned by an honest and public negotiator, were not the result of bribery.[b]

To calculate the "extraordinary" profit and the damages, the court took into consideration testimonies provided by shipping experts to determine the difference between the amounts actually paid by Fyffes and the amounts that would have been paid, all things being equal, if Fyffes had been represented in the negotiations by an honest and prudent broker, rather than a corrupt employee.[c]

Note: Fyffes Group Ltd. v. Templeman [2000] 2 Lloyd's Rep 643 (U.K.).
a. OECD/World Bank, *Identification and Quantification of the Proceeds of Bribery*, rev. ed., p. 56, February 2012, OECD Publishing, http://dx.doi.org/10.1787/9789264174801-en.
b. Ibid., 57.
c. Ibid.

all contractual fees already paid in application of the contract and that the contractor could not recover unpaid fees or the value of the work done, as shown by the case described in box 7.3.

In other cases, however, courts have declined restitution of the full value of a contract obtained through bribes if the government benefited from the contract. Instead, the state may be awarded the contract price minus any benefits that it has received. In addition, contracts may contain clauses imposing penalty or liquidated damages in cases where a party does not respect its own obligations, including noncorruption clauses (see box 7.4).

BOX 7.2	Reputational and Moral Damages Caused by Corruption: Case of the City of Cannes against Ex-Mayor and Bribers

After they were convicted of corruption for taking bribes, the City of Cannes sued the mayor of Cannes and the bribe payers. Both the mayor and the bribe payers were found liable and ordered to pay the city €100,000 for the town's loss of reputation caused by the wrongdoing, on top of other fines in respect of their criminal convictions.

The bribe payers appealed the decision, which was confirmed by the *Cour d'appel* of Aix en Provence on December 14, 2005. Before the *Cour de Cassation* (the highest French judicial court), the bribe payers tried to argue that civil remedies did not apply. They argued that the harm of a public person is attached to the general "*intérêt social,*" which is protected by the action of the state, the criminal action, and that therefore civil damages should not apply.

The *Cour de cassation* rejected that argument and followed the lower court, stating: "the corruption of its mayor, carried out under the suspects' instructions, had highly damaged the good reputation of this city especially known worldwide for its movie festival and its other international events." It also affirmed the *Cour d'appel* in awarding civil compensation to the City of Cannes, which was shared jointly by the mayor and the bribers, on the ground that corruption and complicity were associated offenses.

To reach this conclusion, the *Cour de cassation* said that the *Cour d'appel* had properly found that moral damages were suffered by the City of Cannes, which is distinct from the damage to the society, against the *intérêt social* covered by the criminal fines.

Note: Cour d'appel d'Aix en Provence, December 14, 2005, confirmed by Cour de cassation, March 14, 2007, n° de pourvoi 06-81010.

BOX 7.3	Recovery of the Total Amount of the Corrupt Contract: *S. T. Grand Inc. v. City of New York* (United States)

The Grand company had entered into a contract with the City of New York worth US$840,000 to clean a reservoir. Grand had received US$690,000 and was owed the remaining US$150,000. It was then exposed that the contract had been awarded through the payment of a kickback to a city official.

Grand sued the city for the unpaid balance; the city counterclaimed to recover the amount it had already paid. The highest court of New York applied the general rule that where work is done pursuant to an illegal municipal contract, no recovery may be had by the vendor, either on the contract or in quantum meruit. Thus, Grand was ordered to forgo the entire amount of the contract, approximately US$840,000.

Note: S. T. Grand Inc. v. City of New York 32 N.Y.2d 300, 298 N.E.2d 105 N.Y. 1973, at 108.

Transnet entered into maintenance agreements with Cameroon Airlines, a state-owned company. Through an intermediary, bribes were paid to senior Cameroon Airlines personnel and government officials.

An arbitral tribunal ruled that Cameroon Airlines could void the contracts but could not obtain restitution for the total amount it had paid under the contracts. Cameroon Airlines was entitled to restitution of the sums paid in application of corrupted maintenance agreements minus the "fair value" of services provided by Transnet. This "fair value" deduction from the amount paid consisted of the commercial price, less the "commission" added by Transnet to recoup the bribes paid to Cameroon Airlines' employees.[a] The tribunal held that "where an innocent party to a contract tainted by bribery seeks restitution of that which he has performed South African law requires that it must make or tender restitution of that which it has received or if this is not possible tender a monetary substitution of such benefits instead."[b]

On appeal, the U.K. High Court of Justice annulled the award for procedural reasons, but it agreed with the tribunal that Cameroon Airlines was not entitled to the full contract price because Transnet could exclude its own cost of rendering the services from restitution.

Note: Cameroon Airlines v. Transnet Ltd. [2004] APP.L.R. 07/29.
a. A joint OECD/StAR analysis, *Identification and Quantification of the Proceeds of Bribery* (2011), 37, http://www.oecd.org/daf/anti-bribery/50057547.pdf.
b. Cameroon Airlines v. Transnet Ltd. [2004] APP.L.R. 07/29 para 123.

3. Accounting for Profits or Disgorgement

Remedies based on unjust enrichment, including disgorgement, are based on the principle that no one should benefit from his own wrongdoing. Accordingly a court may force wrongdoers to give up profits obtained illegally, plus interest, to prevent unjust enrichment.

Under certain circumstances, profits that a bribe payer earns from a tainted contract will be awarded to the state. In some jurisdictions, the starting point for calculating the benefits to be "disgorged" or accounted for is the gross or net revenues generated by the contract.

It is helpful to illustrate the calculation by using the example of actions by civil regulators against corruption. One such approach is "disgorgement" of profits wrongfully obtained.[6] In such cases, a common method is the *net revenue method.* The damages are

---

6. These methods are used by the United States Securities and Exchange Commission in its civil enforcement proceedings.

BOX 7.5	Example of the Net Revenue Method

Proceeds = Net revenues (gross revenues from the contract minus costs/expenses)

In a hypothetical *Sales of Goods and Services Case,* in return for bribes amounting to US$5 million, a company obtained projects to build communications networks and control systems for state-owned enterprises. The revenues from the projects were valued at US$100 million. The company paid US$25 million for the goods sold for the projects. The company also disguised the bribes as a legitimate expense in its books and records, and deducted the expense from its taxes.

Calculating the benefit (in U.S. dollars)

The benefit subject to confiscation was calculated using the "net revenue" method:

	Revenues received from projects:	$100,000,000
−	Cost of goods sold for projects:	$25,000,000
+	Total amount of bribes paid:	$5,000,000
=	Total benefit derived:	$80,000,000

Note: A joint OECD/StAR analysis, *Identification and Quantification of the Proceeds of Bribery* (2011), 31, http://www.oecd.org/daf/anti-bribery/50057547.pdf.

the gross contract revenues, minus certain legitimate costs or expenses incurred by the briber in executing the contract. Deductions could include, for example, the cost of supplying goods and services.[7]

Another method, the *additional profit method*, would produce different outcomes. It calculates the profits that would have been made if no bribery had occurred. Thus, one would need to compare similar contracts where no bribery occurred, to the contract involving bribery, and calculate the differences.[8] A third approach would be to demand the *gross profits*, which in effect is asking for the de facto invalidation of the contract.

4. Specific Challenges Encountered in Quantifying Restitutions

In net revenue calculations, some particular complications result from the need to identify deductible costs attributable to the specific corrupt contract. Materials purchased or staff hired to fulfill the contract are generally considered as variable costs that can be deducted. More problematic are fixed costs that the company incurs, such as buildings or permanent staff and management who spend only part of their time

---

7. OECD/World Bank, *Identification and Quantification of the Proceeds of Bribery*, rev. ed., 30.
8. Ibid., 32.

working on the contract tainted by bribery. Although the method of allocating these costs is clearly defined in many businesses, there will always be an element of judgment in determining whether such fixed costs can be allocated to a specific contract. As a result, governments or other entities seeking to recover assets may need assistance from accounting experts to be able to present arguments to the court.

Similarly, in the damages phase of litigation, detailed analysis from accounting as well as technical experts may be necessary to determine the "ordinary" market rates or profit margin of the goods or services that were inflated by the contractor with the assistance of a corrupt official. In addition, compensation claims may require the calculation of interest income earned by the briber, or lost by the claimant, on amounts awarded as damages. When lengthy time periods are considered, the determination of applicable interest rates and the periods over which the interest is calculated will be crucial.

More generally, some jurisdictions still lack legislation dealing with civil redress. Others may have legislation in place that has never been tested in practice; they may consider calculations regarding profits obtained and damages suffered as too complicated. Only a few courts have addressed such issues; judges have very little experience and thus will need to be patiently educated by skilled counsel. Even when countries have both adequate legislation in place and courts that are used to dealing with quantification issues, it is frequently difficult to identify the proceeds of corruption and calculate the profits because of the secrecy involved in corrupt practices, especially when the bribery is revealed years after the contract has been awarded.

B. Beyond the Present—Emerging Theories

Practitioners should bear in mind that for some companies, paying out funds to settle civil claims or compensate a victim may be perceived as a necessary business expense.[9] Given the low probability of being caught, a company that engages in corrupt practices, and is consistently awarded government contracts, may consider that being ordered to disgorge profits or to compensate damages resulting from a single transaction is just the price it pays for making money later. In other words, paying damages could be viewed as an investment. In that context, penalties may act as deterrents only if they are a multiple of actual damages.[10] Punitive damages would also motivate private plaintiffs to go to court because the damage awards would be far greater.

The issues raised by punitive damages warrant more specific discussions and go beyond the limits of this study. In tort litigation, punitive damages are common in the United States, where some types of lawsuits (for example, antitrust violations and False Claims Act claims) routinely subject defendants to paying triple the amount of the actual

---

9. Indeed, it may be deductible from their taxes as a business expense.
10. Susan Rose-Ackerman and Paul D. Carrington, *Anti-Corruption Policy: Can International Actors Play a Constructive Role?* (Durham, NC: Carolina Academic Press, 2013).

In the case of the *County of San Bernardino et al. v. Kenneth Walsh et al.*, which involved two bribery schemes, the court of appeals held that "the proper measure of damages is full disgorgement of any secret profit made by the fiduciary regardless of whether the principal suffered any damage."[a] On the claims other than unfair competition, the court awarded actual damages of US\$4.2 million, comprising the bribe-taker's salary, direct bribes to him, other kickbacks, and a corrupt agent's consulting fees. The court also awarded US\$1 million in punitive damages against one corrupt official, and US\$500,000 in punitive damages against the corrupt agent of the bribe-paying company, on the breach of fiduciary and fraud causes of action.

The appeals court upheld the award of punitive damages, finding it was justified by the reprehensibility of the defendants' conduct and was reasonably based on the relationship between the punitive damages award, the compensatory damages award, and the harm done; and the amount of the award in proportion to each defendant's net worth.[b]

Note: County of San Bernardino v. Walsh 158 Cal. App. 4th 533, 69 Cal. Rptr. 3d 848 (Cal. App. 2 Dist. 2007).
a. Ibid. at 542.
b. Ibid. at 545.

damage (box 7.6). By contrast, most European states view damages as a "compensatory instrument" and oppose a system that would result in damages that are higher than the loss sustained by the victim.[11] Moreover, damage multipliers of a punitive nature are often viewed as inconsistent with the principles of compensation that should motivate civil claims, and for that reason are viewed as contradictory to public policy (*ordre public*, in French).

The concept of environmental and social damages has also emerged recently, notably in some jurisdictions in Central and South America. A "social damage" may be defined as the loss that is incurred not only by specific groups or individuals but by the community as a whole. It could include damage to the environment, to the credibility of institutions, or to collective rights such as health, security, peace, education, good governance, and good public financial management. Social damage is different from damages to collective rights that belong to a restricted and identifiable group of individuals or legal entities. Social damage can be pecuniary and nonpecuniary (box 7.7).

---

11. See Commission of the European Communities, "Commission Staff Working Paper, Accompanying the White Paper on Damages Actions for Breach of the EC Antitrust Rules," § 182 (2008); http://eur-lex.europa.eu/LexUriServ/LexUriServ.do?uri=SEC:2008:0404:FIN:EN:PDF.

BOX 7.7 **The Notion of Social Damages to Obtain Full Compensation: The Example of Costa Rica**

In Costa Rica, Alcatel-Lucent and individual defendants were charged with paying bribes to government officials, political parties, and officials of the state-owned telecom company, *Instituto Costarricense de Electricidad* (ICE), to secure cellular network contracts.

The attorney general's Office for Public Ethics, acting as a victim of this offense, sought compensation for the social damage caused by Alcatel-Lucent to the people and the Treasury of Costa Rica and for the loss of prestige suffered by the nation of Costa Rica. The attorney general filed a claim based on Article 38 of the Costa Rican Criminal Procedural Code (CPC), which states that civil action for social harm may be brought by the attorney general's office in the case of offenses involving collective or diffuse interests. Thus, based on the criminal law, the Costa Rican law gives the attorney general's office, acting as a victim, the ability to launch a civil action to seek reparation for social damage.

In its claim, the attorney general's office underlined that the Costa Rican Constitutional Court had previously defined as "collective and diffuse interests" the "citizen's collective interest in good public finance management" and "the inhabitant's right to a healthy environment."

To measure the social damages, the office of the attorney general hired an external consultant to estimate damages using a methodology combining the following elements:

- Economic consequences of corruption, which reduced investors' trust in the Costa Rican government

- Political consequences, which reduced the credibility of politicians and political parties and thus affected (by increasing) the number of abstentions in the elections of 2006

To quantify these consequences, experts used a combination of quantitative analysis and survey data on citizens' perceptions to explain and measure the impact.

However, establishing causality, both to provide evidence of immaterial social damage and to measure that damage, proved challenging. For example, it was difficult to define what would have been the level of trust in the Costa Rican government in the absence of Alcatel's corrupt activities. It was similarly complex to quantify the economic consequences of the loss of trust alleged by prosecutors.

In addition, a precedent-setting case involving bribery and kickbacks in the purchase of medical equipment for the social security system in Costa Rica had previously highlighted the challenges inherent in the concept of social damage. In that case, the attorney general's office had sought compensation for social

(continued next page)

BOX 7.7   (*continued*)

damages, estimated to be around US$89 million, but the court dismissed the evidence.

Given the difficulties, the attorney general accepted a settlement agreement, signed within the civil proceedings, by which the claims for social damage were dismissed and Alcatel agreed to pay US$10 million.

Note: See Juanita Olaya, Kodjo Attisso, and Anja Roth, *Repairing Social Damage out of Corruption Cases: Opportunities and Challenges as Illustrated in the Alcatel Case in Costa Rica* (2010), http://14iacc.org/wp-content/uploads /SocialDamagePaper20.01.2011.pdf.

8. Enforcement and Collection of Judgments

The recognition, enforcement, and collection of a judgment are the last steps in civil proceedings. Yet in cases involving asset recovery, those final steps should be considered at the start, given the challenges of enforcing court orders obtained outside the jurisdiction where the assets are located. Many practitioners would say that a judgment that is not enforceable is not worth the paper on which it is written, and that only judgments that can be executed—that is, translated into action—are meaningful.

But formal enforcement may not be necessary in every case, since consent—agreement to pay—makes it unnecessary. In certain cases, when a civil case is settled by agreement of the parties, an award of damages could be obtained without formal enforcement because the adverse party will have agreed to pay from assets located there or elsewhere.[1] It is also possible that an opposing party will agree to pay some portion of the foreign judgment, in consideration of that party's estimate of the winning state party's chances of enforcing the foreign judgment. In the absence of some kind of agreement, however, formal enforcement will be the only option to achieve collection. This chapter examines the recognition and enforcement of civil judgments in the jurisdiction where assets are located. It also addresses the challenges of collecting judgments.

A. The Recognition and Enforcement of Civil Judgments in an International Context

The claimant will most likely need to enforce his judgment in the country where the assets sought are located. It consists of two steps: first, recognition, and then enforcement. The "recognition" of a judgment means that another court accepts it, without hearing evidence and engaging in an independent decision-making process, and then issues its own judgment stating substantially the same conclusion and terms. "Enforcement" means execution of judgments, that is, collection of the assets or the amount awarded to the plaintiff.

If the judgment and the assets are in the same jurisdiction, there is no need for recognition, because it is a "domestic" rather than "foreign" judgment.[2] In general, recognition

---

1. See box 3.4, in chapter 3, concerning the Alcoa case (settled out of court).
2. In such cases, only enforcement needs to occur. See, for example, box 3.2, in chapter 3, concerning Zambia's successful civil suit against Chiluba in the United Kingdom.

and enforcement of a foreign judgment in a civil matter is a sensitive area, traditionally considered linked to national sovereignty.

Where a judgment creditor (here, the plaintiff state) seeks to enforce a judgment through access to local assets of the judgment debtor, recognition must precede the enforcement of the judgment against the assets. International cooperation by way of multilateral or regional conventions tries to resolve those issues. But whereas international cooperation is widely developed in criminal law, its scope in civil law is still limited. This section gives a brief overview of existing international and regional cooperation for the recognition and enforcement of foreign judgments in civil matters. It will then focus on the procedural law governing the matter.

1. International Cooperation Regarding the Recognition and Enforcement of Foreign Civil Asset Recovery Judgments

There is no treaty with a global reach that governs the enforcement of foreign civil judgments.[3] Civil judgments can be enforced between jurisdictions through processes such as reciprocal enforcement of judgments (sometimes called "comity") and related laws. To resolve the international cooperation issue in terms of enforcement, states have created a patchwork, signing multilateral and bilateral treaties and sometimes offering regional responses.

Multilateral Conventions to Enforce Civil Judgments for Asset Recovery

Certain conventions deal with the enforcement of foreign judgments in civil matters:

- **The 1971 Hague Convention on the Recognition and Enforcement of Foreign Judgments in Civil and Commercial Matters.** The convention is a multilateral treaty governing the mutual recognition and enforcement of judicial decisions rendered in civil or commercial matters. Article 4 provides that a decision rendered in one of the contracting states shall be entitled to recognition and enforcement in another contracting state, provided that it was given by a court that had jurisdiction and is no longer subject to review in the state of origin. Article 5 provides the grounds for refusal of the enforcement of a court decision, such as public policy arguments, fraud, and *res judicata*. To be enforceable in the state addressed, a decision must be enforceable in the state of origin; there can be no review of the merits of the decision rendered by the court of origin.[4] As of today very few states are signatories to the convention, which limits its scope. An ongoing project known as the "Judgments Project" might bring interesting outcomes. Under the Hague Conference on Private International Law, the Council of General Affairs and Policy, composed of all members, established

---

3. In contrast to court judgments, an exception is the New York Arbitration Convention, which governs the recognition and enforcement of foreign arbitral awards.
4. Article 8 of the 1971 Hague Convention on the Recognition and Enforcement of Foreign Judgments in Civil and Commercial Matters.

a working group to prepare a "Judgments Project" that will include proposals on the recognition and enforcement of judgments, including jurisdictional filters.[5]

- **The United Nations Convention Against Corruption (UNCAC).** UNCAC encourages cooperation for enforcement of civil decisions but does not include compulsory provisions. Under the chapter related to international cooperation, legal assistance between states is mandatory in criminal matters but is optional with regard to civil matters. UNCAC provides solely for assistance in civil and administrative proceedings, requiring that state parties permit civil suits by other state parties in their national courts and similarly, that state parties recognize judgments of other state party courts.

- **The Civil Law Convention on Corruption.** Within the Council of Europe, the signatories parties to the Civil Law Convention on Corruption are required to cooperate effectively in matters relating to civil proceedings in cases of corruption, especially concerning jurisdiction, recognition, and enforcement of foreign judgments (Article 13).[6]

Regional Approaches

The European Union (EU) and other European countries have adopted a well-defined regional approach to tackle the problem of recognition and enforcement of civil judgments rendered abroad.

To ensure the economic development of the EU, a mechanism to ensure that judgments of the courts in Europe are enforceable on a uniform basis was a logical necessity.[7] The "Brussels regime," as the EU approach is known, facilitates the free circulation of judgments and ensures access to justice by giving jurisdiction and enforcement of judgments to foreign judges within member states in civil matters.

- **The European Enforcement Order for uncontested claims.** The European Enforcement Order (EEO) is a certificate for uncontested claims that accompanies a judgment, a court settlement, or an authentic instrument and allows that judgment, settlement, or instrument to circulate freely in the EU.[8] A creditor with an

---

5. The "Judgments Project" refers to the work undertaken by the Hague Conference since 1992 on two key aspects of private international law in cross-border litigation in civil and commercial matters: the international jurisdiction of courts and the recognition and enforcement of their judgments abroad. See Hague Conference on Private International Law, "Judgments Projects," available at http://www.hcch.net/index_en.php?act=text.display&tid=149.

6. Civil Law Convention on Corruption, Article 13—International co-operation: "The Parties shall co-operate effectively in matters relating to civil proceedings in cases of corruption, especially concerning the service of documents, obtaining evidence abroad, jurisdiction, recognition and enforcement of foreign judgments and litigation costs, in accordance with the provisions of relevant international instruments on international co-operation in civil and commercial matters to which they are Party, as well as with their internal law." The convention is available at http://conventions.coe.int/Treaty/en/Treaties/Html/174.htm.

7. Shelby R. Grubbs, *International Civil Procedure*, World Law Group Series (The Hague: Kluwer Law International, 2003).

8. The EEO was established by EC Regulation No. 804/2004 of April 21, 2004, and entered into force on October 21, 2005.

EEO can enforce a judgment in another European Union state without needing to undertake any other court proceedings or a declaration of enforceability in the member state.[9]

- **Council Regulation (EC) 1215/2012/EU of December 12, 2012, on jurisdiction and the recognition and enforcement of judgments in civil and commercial matters.**[10] Based on mutual trust in the administration of justice, certain regulations recognized that a judgment rendered in any EU member state and enforceable in that state was enforceable in the other member states without any special procedure being required.[11] These changes abolished the former *exequatur* procedure. As a result, it is not necessary to address a declaration of enforceability prior to enforcement in the member state. The principle of direct enforcement of civil judgments within the EU will be applied, and a judgment given by the courts of a member state will be treated as if it has been given in another member state. However, the person against whom enforcement is sought can apply for refusal of recognition or enforcement of a judgment if he considers that one of the grounds for refusal of recognition applies.

- **The Lugano Convention on Jurisdiction and the Enforcement of Judgments in Civil and Commercial Matters.**[12] The objective of the Lugano Convention is to ensure that judgments rendered in one contracting state are recognized in any other contracting state, without any special procedure required (box 8.1). The Lugano Convention is a parallel convention to the Brussels Regulation. The signatories are the members of the European Union and the European Free Trade Association members with the exception of Liechtenstein.[13]

Other Regional approaches tend to be more limited.

- **The Inter-American Convention on the Extraterritorial Validity of Foreign Judgments and Arbitral Awards.** This convention establishes rules that address the recognition and enforcement of foreign judgments among its members. It applies only when there is an existing judgment or arbitral award rendered in

---

9. Ibid. Article 3 of the regulation defines uncontested claims.

10. Full text available at http://eur-lex.europa.eu/LexUriServ/LexUriServ.do?uri=OJ:L:2012:351:0001:0032 :EN:PDF.

11. Regulation No. 44/2001. On December 22, 2000, the council adopted Regulation (EC) No. 44/2001, which replaces the 1968 Brussels Convention. This regulation unified the rules of conflict of jurisdiction in civil and commercial matters and simplified the formalities, with a view to rapid and simple recognition and enforcement of judgments within the European Union. Regulation (EU) 1215/2012/ EU, of the European Parliament and of the council, adopted on December 12, 2012, which will enter into force on January 10, 2015, recasts and repeals the former Council Regulation No. 44/2001, of December 22, 2000, on Jurisdiction and the Recognition and Enforcement of Judgments in Civil and Commercial Matters.

12. The Lugano Convention on Jurisdiction and the Enforcement of Judgments in Civil and Commercial Matters, OJ L 339, 21.12.2007.

13. Switzerland, Iceland, Denmark, and Norway.

civil, commercial, or labor proceedings in one of the signatory countries.[14] In such cases, the convention sets forth the requirements that must be met to establish the extraterritorial validity of such judgments and the procedures to recognize and enforce them.[15] The convention is in force in the following countries (among others): Argentina, Bolivia, Brazil, Colombia, Ecuador, Mexico, Paraguay, Peru, Uruguay, and Venezuela.

- **Protocol of Las Leñas on Jurisdictional Cooperation and Assistance in Civil, Commercial, Labor, and Administrative Matters.**[16] The Protocol of Las Leñas applies to Mercosur member states, Bolivia, and Chile. It establishes a mechanism for circulation of civil judgments through central authorities.[17] This mechanism gives victim states an alternative to the costly procedures of enforcing judgments abroad (by hiring local attorneys, etc.). This type of instrument may prove valuable, especially to facilitate the enforcement of judgments in favor of developing countries.

In the absence of an applicable convention, the recognition and enforcement of foreign civil judgments is largely dictated by the enforcing state's own procedural law. Countries can choose whether to recognize a foreign judgment or not, following their own procedures.

Provisional measures regarding the preservation of assets, such as worldwide freezing orders, are no exception. They are enforced as foreign civil judgments, as illustrated by the case described in box 8.1, concerning the enforceability in Switzerland of a worldwide freezing order.

2. Enforcement of Judgments as Part of the Legal Strategy in Foreign Civil Asset Recovery Cases

As with the choice of forum, procedural strategies come into play regarding the enforcement of civil judgments. As noted above, the likelihood of enforcement in the foreign court is one of the elements to consider in deciding where to initiate civil

---

14. The Inter-American Convention on the Extraterritorial Validity of Foreign Judgments and Arbitral Awards was adopted in 1979 in Montevideo among the Organization of American States (OAS) states and subsequently clarified and complemented by the Inter-American Convention on Jurisdiction in the International Sphere for the Extraterritorial Validity of Foreign Judgments, in 1984.

15. Dra Mariana Silveira, "Jurisdiction-Fundamental concepts: Focus on Latin America", National Law Center for Inter-American Free Trade, September 2000, available at http://www.ilpf.org/events/jurisdiction2/presentations/silveira_pr/silveira.htm.

16. Decision No 5/92, Valle de Las Leñas, June 27, 1992, and Complementary Agreement, Decision No. 5/97, Buenos Aires, June 19, 1997, *Protocolo de Cooperación y Asistencia Jurisdiccional en Materia Civil, Comercial, Laboral y Administrativa. Decisión No. 5/92, firmado en el Valle de Las Leñas, el 27 de junio de 1992;* available at www.mercosur.org.uy/espanol/snor/normativa/decisiones/DEC592.HTM; and *Acuerdo Complementario al Protocolo de Cooperación y Asistencia Jurisdiccional en Materia Civil, Comercial, Laboral y Administrativa, Decisión No 5/97, firmado en Asunción, el 19 de junio de 1997;* available at www.mercosur.org.uy/espanol/snor/normativa/decisiones/DEC0597.HTM.

17. See Chapter 5 of the protocol.

BOX 8.1 **Enforcing a Worldwide Freezing Order Issued by a Foreign Court: A Decision of the Swiss Federal Supreme Court**

The Supreme Court of Switzerland had to address the enforceability in Switzerland of a worldwide freezing order (WFO) from the London High Court of Justice. Provisional measures regarding the preservation of assets are generally enforceable in Switzerland, under certain conditions.

Following the Swiss procedural law, according to which a party seeking declaratory relief must in principle demonstrate that it has an actual interest in obtaining it, the Zurich Appeal Court imposed an additional condition that the applicant show "a legitimate interest," in order to obtain the declaration of enforceability of the WFO in Switzerland. If the party could later be compensated monetarily, the courts would generally deny that such interest exists. The Zurich Court of Appeal also considered that although the WFO was not legally binding on third parties on Swiss territory, banks usually comply voluntarily with a foreign freezing order. It thus concluded that a declaration of enforceability would not be of any use to the claimant.

The claimants successfully appealed to the Swiss Federal Supreme Court, which held that a party is not required to show a legitimate interest to obtain a declaration of enforceability of a freezing order. It further held that the Swiss banks' voluntary compliance with a foreign freezing order is irrelevant to the claimants' right to have the order declared enforceable.[a] Once the claimant obtains such a declaration, the foreign freezing order is treated as if it were a Swiss decision. Once a foreign judgment is recognized, it should be treated equally with domestic judgments. Thus, once declared enforceable by domestic courts, the judgment can be enforced.[b]

Note: Swiss Federal Supreme Court (4A_366/2011), October 31, 2011.
a. Simone Nadelhofer and Sandrine Giroud, "Enforcement of Worldwide Freezing Orders in Switzerland," *International Bar Association, International Litigation Newsletter* (2012), http://www.lalive.ch/data/publications/SGI+SNA-IBA-Enforcement_of _WFO_in_Switzerland_Int_Litigation.pdf.
b. See Matthias Scherer and Simone Nadelhofer. "Possible enforcement of Worldwide Freezing Orders in Switzerland", kluwer Arbitration Blog, March 23, 2012, available at http://kluwerarbitrationblog.com/blog/2012/03/23/possible-enforcement -of-worldwide-freezing-orders-in-switzerland/.

proceedings. States and other relevant entities that are victims of corruption wishing to recover stolen assets through civil actions will often be reluctant to initiate proceedings in the country where the corrupt act(s) took place, if those countries are not parties to international conventions regarding the enforcement and recognition of judgments (box 8.2).

Additionally, some jurisdictions are more willing to enforce a judgment from certain countries than others because of due process concerns and requirements to respect public policies.

| BOX 8.2 | More on the Case of Chiluba: *Attorney General of Zambia v. Meer Care and Desai & Ors* (United Kingdom) |

The basic facts of a related case are described in box 3.2, in chapter 3. The case of Chiluba provides a good example of the importance of considering enforceability when deciding where to bring a case. While pursuing criminal actions in Zambia, the Zambian authorities also began a private civil lawsuit in the United Kingdom in 2004. A civil action before British courts offered the best hope of recovering some of the laundered money. The advantage of having orders issued by English courts rather than a Zambian court was the greater likelihood of enforceability of orders—also considering that the United Kingdom is party to the Brussels regime. Zambia enforced the judgments, recovering large sums.

Note: Attorney General of Zambia v. Meer Care and Desai & Ors [2007] EWHC 952 (Ch).

If the court asked to recognize the foreign judgment has doubts about whether that judgment was rendered by an impartial tribunal and in compliance with due process, that court is unlikely to recognize the foreign judgment. For example, if it is not clear that the defendants had notice and an opportunity to be heard at all stages, chances of recognition will be low. A similar result could be expected if a credible argument could be made that any kind of fraud tainted the foreign proceedings.

Defendants can be expected to, and will, make such arguments through competent counsel. Thus, these factors must be considered at the outset. Even though it may be relatively easy to obtain a judgment in one jurisdiction as compared to another, it may not be worth it if, for example, the courts in that country have a poor reputation for following the rule of law and respecting rights.

Even *ex ante* at the outset of a case, the likely difficulty of enforcing a judgment from one country may cause a court in another country to be more likely to assert jurisdiction rather than force the plaintiff to go obtain a judgment from that country. Courts are fundamentally concerned with fairness and may be reluctant to send a plaintiff off to another court where the ultimate result may thwart enforcement (box 8.3). The importance accorded to enforcement in civil asset recovery cases is also illustrated by the case in box 8.4.

B. The Challenges of Collecting Civil Judgments

Once a civil judgment is obtained (domestically or in a foreign venue), recognized, and enforced by the foreign courts, it still has to be collected. A successful plaintiff may face unwilling defendants, and if that is the case, the collection process may be complex and costly. Efforts to collect a judgment may also be frustrated if the defendant has become insolvent during the litigation, or has secreted his assets,

BOX 8.3	Difficulty of Enforcement in Nigeria Supports U.K. Court's Decision to Keep Case in the United Kingdom: More on *Federal Republic of Nigeria v. Joshua Dariye & Another* (United Kingdom)

As illustrated in box 3.1, in chapter 3 (*Federal Republic of Nigeria v. Joshua Dariye & Another*), the ease of enforcing a judgment is a factor in the choice of forum. The defendant Dariye argued the case should be heard in his native Nigeria, and the plaintiff state of Nigeria opposed. In the case of Dariye, the court examined whether it would be difficult to enforce a judgment obtained in Nigeria in relation to bank accounts found in England and took into account that a Nigerian court would have problems obtaining disclosure from English banks.

Source: World Bank.

BOX 8.4	Kuwaiti Investment Organization/Sheikh Fahad Mohammed al-Sabah (United Kingdom)

During a period of four years, between 1989 and 1992, the Kuwaiti government was the victim of theft, misappropriation, and embezzlement. The Kuwaiti Investment Office (KIO), as part of the Kuwait Investment Authority (a governmental investment organization), lost US$5 billion from its investments in Spain through the KIO's London offices.

Approximately US$1.2 billion was considered missing and unaccounted for (that is, stolen, embezzled, or misappropriated). It was suspected that the missing money had been taken by some of the top KIO management officials, including members of the royal family managing the office. Banks, accountants, and lawyers were also considered defendants.

The KIO filed private civil actions in the United Kingdom against both institutions and individuals. The KIO won a civil judgment in the U.K. against Sheikh Fahad Mohammed Al-Sabah, a member of the Kuwaiti royal family and chairman of KIO from 1984 to 1992. KIO later sought enforcement of the U.K. judgment in the Bahamas, where Sheikh Fahad was a resident, and in Jersey and the Cayman Islands, where he held assets through trusts over which he held control.

Note: Contribution of Dr. Mohammad A. A. Al Moqatei, *Stolen Asset Recovery: A Good Practices Guide for Non-Conviction Based Asset Forfeiture*, http://www.coe.int/t/dghl/monitoring/moneyval/web_ressources/IBRDWB_Guidassetrecovery.pdf.

or fraudulently transferred them to third persons.[18] It can be an even more difficult process when a judgment issued by a court has to be collected on assets hidden in another jurisdiction. Some legal mechanisms exist for the collection of judgment debts, so-called execution procedures. That being said, the difficulty of enforcing a

---

18. It should be noticed, however, that insolvency procedures can also offer advantages in the Asset recovery process; see in chapter 9, "Using Insolvency or Similar Proceedings in Asset Recovery Cases"

civil debt (as compared to a criminal one) might represent a challenge and a significant cost in asset recovery cases.

1. The Role of Execution Procedures

Civil execution procedures are the coercive measures that a judgment creditor may take against his debtor to recover a claim established by an enforcement order or to recover his property. If a defendant pays the verdict voluntarily, execution is unnecessary.

By using execution procedures, however, plaintiffs may force unwilling defendants to pay their debts. Execution applies to both personal and real property. In bribery and money laundering cases, most of the wealth corruptly acquired is generally transferred abroad, making the process of locating and collecting assets particularly complicated and burdensome. Each country has its own legal system in place regarding how to execute a foreign judgment (box 8.5).

BOX 8.5 | Overview of the Execution Procedures in the United States, the United Kingdom, France, and Germany[a]

- In the United States, execution of judgments for the payment of money is governed by Rule 69 of the Federal Rules of Civil Procedure. Once a foreign judgment is recognized in a U.S. court judgment, the U.S. Marshals Service can employ writs of execution to enforce judgments. A writ of execution is a court order, in the form of a final process designed to enforce a money judgment, directing an officer of the court to seize the property of a judgment debtor and transfer the proceeds over to the judgment creditor. When issuing a writ of execution, a court typically will order a sheriff or other similar official to take possession of property owned by a judgment debtor. Such property will often then be sold in a sheriff's sale and the proceeds remunerated to the plaintiff in partial or full satisfaction of the judgment. It is generally considered preferable for the sheriff simply to take possession of money from the defendant's bank account.[b]

- In the United Kingdom, Part 5 of the Proceeds of Crime Act (POCA) of 2002 deals with the recovery of the proceeds of unlawful conduct through proceedings in the civil courts. The whole point is that the Crown does not have to show that the defendants have been convicted of any criminal offense in order to succeed. If the court is satisfied that any property is recoverable, the court must then make a recovery order. The recovery order must vest the recoverable property in a trustee for civil recovery. The functions of the trustee are (a) to secure the detention, custody, or preservation of any property vested in him by the recovery order; (b) in the case of property other than money, to realize the value of the property for the benefit of the enforcement authority. In performing his functions, the trustee acts on behalf of the enforcement authority and must comply with any directions given by the authority.[c]

(continued next page)

- In France, the collection of judgments is regulated by the Code of Civil Execution Procedures, which entered into force on June 1, 2012. Pursuant to this code, a petition has to be submitted through a motion to the executing judge (in French, the *juge de l'execution*), if the claim, because of its nature or amount, falls within the latter's jurisdiction.

In Germany, upon receiving a declaration of enforceability, a garnishment petition for the defendant's moveable assets located in Germany must be filed with the appropriate marshal. As for the immovable assets, a plaintiff can enforce a judgment against the debtor's real property by applying to the local court that has jurisdiction in the matter and will order a sale by court order, forced administration, or registration of a forced mortgage.

Notes:
a. The following descriptions of the execution procedures are purposely simplified.
b. John J. Cound, Jack H. Friedenthal, Arthur R. Miller, and John E. Sexton, *Civil Procedure, Cases and Materials* (Los Angeles: West Group Publishing, 2001).
c. Proceeds of Crime Act 2002, Part 5 Civil recovery of the proceeds etc. of unlawful conduct, Chapter 2 Civil Recovery in the High Court or Court of Session.

In common law countries, in cases where the debtor resists the enforcement and collection of judicial orders, the debtors may expose themselves to contempt of court. Contempt of court is defined as any willful disobedience to, or disregard of, a court order that interferes with a judge's ability to administer justice. Reluctant defendants or third parties (including banks or lawyers) who are notified may be held in contempt of court for failing to comply with such orders or decisions. Possible sanctions include fines, segregation of assets, or a term of imprisonment. Contempt of court is particularly relevant when assets are held offshore. In that context, justice cannot enforce a court order locally, but the defendants expose themselves to contempt of court sanctions. In the United States, for example, coercive civil contempt would most likely occur when a debtor fails to comply with a court order to repatriate money from a foreign trust. As a result, the judge can order imprisonment until the money arrives at the courthouse.[19] The deterrent effect of contempt of court may turn it into a powerful weapon for the enforcement of judgments.

2. The Cost of Collection of Civil Judgments

The high cost of collection may be prohibitive for some developing countries, in view of the ultimate recovery of stolen assets that can be expected. Public authorities may sometimes be reluctant even to initiate civil proceedings, at first, because they anticipate

---

19. Denis A. Kleinfeld, "Contempt—Where the Tyre Meets the Road in Asset Protection," 2009, available at http://www.ifcreview.com/restricted.aspx?articleId=46&areaId=46.

BOX 8.6	A State Enters into a Contract with a Collection Company: A Cautionary Tale of Significant Fees Claimed by a Collection Company Working on Behalf of the Plaintiff State

A government hired the services of an offshore collection company to assist with the recovery of stolen assets. The government had initiated both criminal actions in its own courts and private civil litigation in the United Kingdom to recover assets stolen by corrupt government officials.

A government agency entered into a contract in which it granted the collection company the exclusive right to recover assets misappropriated by government officials. The company asked for a million dollars up-front, plus 20 percent to 50 percent of the recovered funds. Several years later, the government did not pay for services allegedly rendered by the collection agency. As a result, the company brought a claim in arbitration to collect fees for services that the government asserts were neither performed nor received.

Source: World Bank.

complex and costly legal, including collection, processes. As a result, the role of collection agencies is often crucial in cases where the proceeds of transnational corruption are often hidden in foreign jurisdictions using vehicles designed to break the chain of ownership.[20] Resorting to collection companies at the end of the asset recovery process is another cost in addition to legal representation fees, and it can be very costly, as illustrated in box 8.6.

---

20. Abiola Makinwa, "Researching Civil Remedies for International Corruption: The Choice of the Functional Comparative Method," *Erasmus Law Review* 2, no. 3 (2009): 331 et seq.

9. Using Insolvency, Receivership, or Similar Proceedings to Trace or Recover Assets

When an entity was deprived of, or benefited from, stolen assets, it may become bankrupt or insolvent or be placed under receivership or provisional administration. This situation may increase asset recovery opportunities for governments, which may use receivership and other insolvency proceedings to trace and recover assets. The terms "bankruptcy" and "insolvency" are used differently in different legal systems, sometimes interchangeably. Here we use "insolvency" as the overarching term to describe proceedings that are in court, including liquidation and reorganization and similar out-of-court proceedings, including receivership.

A. Purpose of Insolvency or Similar Proceedings

The purpose of insolvency proceedings is to seize and sell assets of the debtor/defendant and distribute the money equitably to creditors, to protect the rights of creditors and injured parties. The first step is usually a moratorium, or freeze, on all transactions. Then the court appoints an administrator with significant powers not only to seize and sell assets, but to investigate and demand information that will help to locate the assets.

Receivership or provisional administration is more informal than insolvency. Receivership, in particular, has been an effective recovery tool for stolen assets. Receivership is a process whereby all property subject to claims is placed under the control of an independent person, the "receiver." The job of the receiver is to run the company or to manage the assets. If a secured creditor is not being paid, or the lender finds the company's management practices dubious, a receiver can be appointed based on a contract between a borrower and a creditor. Court action is not required (box 9.1).

Once the receiver is appointed, they can take over the operations of a company and take custody of all the assets. Thus, the receiver can not only seize the company's assets as necessary to pay the debts but also stop its directors and managers from taking actions detrimental to the company and may be able to stop the misappropriation and dissipation of assets from continuing.

B. Using Insolvency Proceedings in Asset Recovery Cases

If claimed assets are held by an insolvent entity, insolvency laws offer another avenue to recover stolen assets through civil rather than criminal proceedings. Under most insolvency laws, an "insolvency office holder" (frequently referred to as an administrator, liquidator, receiver, or trustee) can be appointed by the court. With regard to the assets to be recovered, insolvency laws authorize the insolvency office holder to take possession of those assets from the individual or company that holds them.

An advantage is that insolvency laws generally give the insolvency office holder powers of discovery and examination of interested parties and third parties that may go beyond those available in other civil approaches. The office holder stands as an officer of the court, or as a fiduciary (guardian of third party monetary interests), rather than an interested party, which is part of the basis of the powers granted to him by law and the courts. Another advantage of insolvency-based recovery is that proof for the purposes of recovery of property or assets under insolvency law is much lower than for a criminal proceeding. In fact, often it is not necessary to prove fraud or bad intent, but rather the assets must only be traced as belonging to the entity in bankruptcy or be shown to have been traded or transferred to the detriment of the creditors. There are also disadvantages, such as relinquishing control to the office holder. The office holder may have different interests.

Receivership is similar but simpler and can be conducted without the participation of a court. In a receivership, a secured creditor, generally a bank, appoints a receiver to take over the assets of a company in order to recover their money. The receiver is empowered to run the business and seize the assets and can be appointed in a short time frame to prevent wastage. The limitations of receivership are that it is available only to the secured creditor of the entity in question, and if a receiver crosses borders, he has less authority than would an officer of the court, such as an administrator.

Insolvency or receivership may present opportunities because the receiver (or other insolvency office holder) enjoys increased powers over assets. In such proceedings, the state claimant may be able to recover property simply by showing that it owns it. It is also easier to reclaim assets that have been transferred away, for example, by fraud. The insolvency office holder has the power to access information and demand testimony and has proved powerful and pivotal in large asset recovery cases.[1] Within an insolvency proceeding, an insolvency office holder can compel the testimony of witnesses, including the directors or managers who may have been culpable in hiding assets.[2] Refusal to cooperate can lead to imprisonment, which may motivate testimony that helps the office holder to locate and subsequently recover substantial assets.

Formal insolvency processes are complex to implement internationally. Generally, in pursuing assets across borders, a plaintiff or creditor will need to pursue the assets under the insolvency laws of that country. Moreover, insolvency judgments are not easily recognized in foreign courts, unless certain regulations, conventions, or model laws apply. Therefore, the insolvency laws of the country where the assets are located will influence the effectiveness of approaching asset recovery through insolvency.

Further analysis is beyond the scope of this study. Suffice it to say that if assets sought are held by an entity in some form of insolvency, there may be some shortcuts on the road to recovery of assets, which could be explored by competent counsel. The description in box 9.2 illustrates how receivership can be used in asset recovery cases.

Box 9.2	Use of a Receiver to Preserve Assets: More on *JSC BTA Bank v. Ablyazov* (United Kingdom)

The basic facts are recounted in box 5.4, in chapter 5. In a complex case with numerous claims, the bank in Kazakhstan sued its former chairman and obtained a freezing order. The bank next applied for a receivership order.

The court had to balance the risk of asset dissipation and the property rights of the defendant, Mr. Ablyazov. The bank supported its request for a receiver with, among other things, (a) the structure used by the defendant, based on nominees who acted for him and the use of corporate structures in jurisdictions "renowned for their secrecy and light regulation"; and (b) the defendant's breach of the freezing order. In this case, the court concluded that it was necessary to appoint a receiver in support of the freezing order to preserve assets and prevent their dissipation prior to trial. The receivership order was designed to enable the receivers to assume control of the corporate structures used.

Note: JSC BTA Bank v. Ablyazov & Ors. [2013] EWCA Civ 928 (England, Court of Appeal, July 25, 2013).

---

1. See Bishopsgate Investment Management Ltd. v. Maxwell (No. 2) [1993] BCLC 814 (United Kingdom).
2. U.K. Insolvency Act 1986, Sections 236 and 366, covering company officials and other business affiliates, and individuals such as the debtor's spouse or other individual that the office holder may suspect has reasonable information.

10. Conclusion

This study on how states may bring private civil lawsuits to recover assets is designed to encourage the development of another legal avenue to pursue stolen assets.

This study is meant to contribute to the rapidly expanding debate on how best to tackle corruption and how to bring more innovative methods to bear. The citizen's cry for justice heard all around the world, from the protests of the Arab Spring to the outrage over the offshore leaks, demands that perpetrators be brought to trial and sentenced, but also that their stolen assets and profits be returned to the victims.

The study endeavors to show how these civil actions can contribute to this objective. To be sure, the amounts of money recovered and repatriated to victim countries so far are not great, and not commensurate with the scale of the theft of public assets and corruption worldwide.

At present, the discipline of asset recovery is still young, and experienced practitioners who can assist countries in charting a course through what is always a very complex and confusing field are few and far between. However, mounting interest in the topic, the G-7 call for transparency, and heightened media scrutiny are improving the situation and coalescing to force action. We hope that some of the tools outlined in the study will provide an additional path to recovering stolen assets.

Appendix A. Glossary

Arbitration. Procedure where the parties agree to resolve a dispute by submitting it to one or more private persons who have no financial interest in the outcome. Arbitration can be used when an international contract provides an arbitration clause or when a bilateral investment treaty provides a basis for investment arbitration.

Assets. Assets of every kind, whether corporeal or incorporeal, movable or immovable, tangible or intangible, and legal documents or instruments evidencing title to or interest in such assets.[1] The term is used interchangeably with **property**.

Balance of probabilities. A fact is more likely than not.

Bona fide purchaser. A third party with an interest in an asset subject to confiscation who did not know of the conduct giving rise to confiscation or, on learning of the conduct giving rise to confiscation, did all that reasonably could be expected under the circumstances to terminate use of the asset. The term is used interchangeably with **innocent owner**.

Bribery. Both the promising, offering, or giving of an undue advantage to a national, international, or foreign public official and the acceptance of an undue advantage by a national public official.

Civil party. In most civil law jurisdictions, a victim of a criminal offense may request the civil party status within the criminal trial against the accused offender. To obtain the civil party status, the victim generally has to show loss or damage resulting directly from the offense. If granted the civil party status, the victim may participate as a civil party in the criminal proceedings and obtain compensation for the harm suffered.

Claimant. The party asserting an interest in the asset. This may include a **third party**, **innocent owner**, **defendant**, or **target**. The term is used interchangeably with **plaintiff**.

Collection (civil debt). Process for recovering delinquent amounts owed.

Compensation. The rule of compensation for the determination of damages is that the victim must be placed in the position it would have been in absent the corruption.

---

1. United Nations Convention Against Corruption (UNCAC), art. 2(e).

Confiscation. The permanent deprivation of assets by order of a court or other competent authority. The term is used interchangeably with **forfeiture**. The persons or entities that hold an interest in the specified funds or other assets at the time of the confiscation lose all rights, in principle, to the confiscated funds or other assets.

Contempt of court. Any willful disobedience to, or disregard of, a court order that interferes with a judge's ability to administer justice.

Contract. A covenant or agreement between two or more persons, with a lawful consideration or cause, to do or abstain from doing some act.[2]

Damages. A pecuniary compensation that may be recovered by a plaintiff for loss, injury, or harm directly caused by a breach of duty, including criminal wrongdoing, immoral conduct, or precontractual fault. The **material damage** (*damnum emergens*) refers to the actual reduction in the economic situation of the person who has suffered the damage. The loss of profits (*lucrum cessans*) represents the profit that could reasonably have been expected but that was not gained because of the vitiated contract or the breach.

Defendant. Any party who is required to answer the complaint of a plaintiff in a civil lawsuit before a court, or any party who has been formally charged or accused of violating a criminal statute.

Disgorgement. Disgorgement is a civil remedy to require the repayment of ill-gotten gains. Unlike confiscation, this remedy is not derived from statute but from the courts' equitable power to correct unjust inequality. It is not meant to be punitive.

Embezzlement. Fraudulent appropriation to his own use or benefit of public funds (property or money) entrusted to him by another, by a clerk, agent, trustee, public officer, or other person acting in a fiduciary character.[3]

Enforcement (civil judgment). Collecting any judgment against an asset held by the defendant up to the value stipulated in the judgment.

Execution procedures. Coercive measures that a judgment creditor may take against his debtor to recover a claim established by an enforcement order or to recover his property.

Forum. Court of justice, or judicial tribunal; a place of jurisdiction; a place where a remedy is sought; a place of litigation.[4]

---

2. *Black's Law Dictionary.*
3. *Black's Law Dictionary.*
4. Ibid.

Informal assistance. Any activity or assistance that is provided without the need for a formal mutual legal assistance (MLA) request. There may be legislation that permits this type of practitioner-to-practitioner assistance, including MLA legislation.

In personam. Latin for "directed toward a particular person." In the context of confiscation or a lawsuit, it is a legal action against a specific person.

In rem. Latin for "against a thing." In the context of confiscation, it is a legal action against a specific thing or asset.

Insolvency. The purpose of insolvency proceedings is to seize and sell assets of the debtor/defendant, and distribute the money equitably to creditors, to protect the rights of creditors and injured parties. "Insolvency" is used in this publication as the overarching term to describe proceedings in court, including liquidation and reorganization and similar out-of-court proceedings, including receivership.

Lawsuit. Private law action between two private persons in the courts of law by which a plaintiff who claims to have incurred loss as a result of a defendant's actions requests legal or equitable remedy. The term is used interchangeably with **civil action**.

Liquidated damages. Clause by which the parties decide when they enter into the contract how much would be paid in the event of a breach of the contract.

Personal claim. Claim against a person that can be satisfied out of various assets. The plaintiff has suffered economic damages and demands to be paid or compensated by the person who caused the damage.

Proprietary claim. Direct claim to a particular piece of property or asset as the true owner. A proprietary claim is a claim that one owns something and asks the court to return that item or equivalent value.

Provisional measure. Temporarily prohibiting the transfer, conversion, disposition, or movement of assets or temporarily assuming custody or control of assets on the basis of an order issued by a court or other competent authority.[5] The term is used interchangeably with **freezing**, **restraint**, **seizure**, and **blocking**.

Punitive damages. The costs that are awarded to a person due to negligence that has caused personal injury or damage to personal property. It is more than the item is worth but considerably so. It is a payment by the person to the injured party as a punishment for reckless behavior.[6]

Receivership. Process where all property subject to claims is placed under the control of an independent person, the "receiver." The job of the receiver is to run the company

---

5. Adapted from UNCAC, art. 2(f).
6. *Black's Law Dictionary*.

or to manage the assets. If a secured creditor is not being paid, or the lender finds the company's management practices dubious, a receiver can be appointed based on a contract between a borrower and a creditor. Court action is not required.

Recognition (civil judgment). Another court accepts a foreign judgment without hearing evidence and engaging in an independent decision-making process, and then issues its own judgment stating substantially the same conclusion and terms.

Restitution. Amount to pay by court order (a) to return an item to the legal owner, (b) for restoration of damaged property to original state, or (c) for victim compensation.[7]

Restraint order. A form of mandatory injunction issued by a judge or a court that restrains any person from dealing with or disposing of the assets named in the order, pending the determination of confiscation proceedings. Court authorization is generally required, but some jurisdictions permit restraint to be ordered by prosecutors or other law enforcement authorities.

Seizure. Taking physical possession of the targeted asset. Court orders are generally required, but some law enforcement agencies in certain jurisdictions are granted the right to seize assets.

Social damage. The loss incurred not only by specific groups or individuals but by the community as a whole.

Tort. Civil wrong, giving rise to a claim for damages.

Tracing. The process by which a claimant demonstrates what has happened to his property, identifies its proceeds, and justifies his claim that the proceeds can properly be regarded as representing his property.[8]

Unjust enrichment. Principle according to which a person should not be permitted to unjustly enrich himself at the expense of another, but should be required to make restitution for property or benefits unjustly received.

Witness. Someone who, either voluntarily or under compulsion, provides testimonial evidence, either oral or written, of what he or she knows or claims to know about a matter, before a court or an official authorized to take such testimony.[9]

---

7. *Black's Law Dictionary.*
8. Foskett v. McKeown and others [2001] 1 A.C. 102 (H.L.) (Eng.), describing tracing as neither a claim nor a remedy but merely a "process."
9. Evidence provided by witnesses, including expert witnesses, is frequently very important in asset recovery cases in both criminal and civil proceedings.

Appendix B. Case Studies

1. Case of Mr. Diepreye Solomon Peter Alamieyeseigha (United Kingdom)

In September 2005, Mr. Alamieyeseigha, governor of Bayelsa state (Nigeria) from May 1999 until his impeachment in 2005, was arrested by the U.K. police on three counts of money laundering. The U.K. Metropolitan Police obtained a wealth of evidence of Mr. Alamieyeseigha's corrupt activities in Nigeria and the laundering of the proceeds internationally. In parallel, Nigeria was also trying to prosecute him for these offenses in its national court and was planning on bringing civil proceedings abroad.

Nigeria wished to move forward with civil lawsuits as well. To do that, Nigeria needed the evidence from the U.K. authorities. The Metropolitan Police had obtained that evidence using its compulsory powers. The police owed duties of confidence to the owners of the documents, which prevented them from voluntarily providing the documents to Nigeria and its lawyers for use in the civil proceedings. To overcome this obstacle, Nigeria applied (without notice to Mr. Alamieyeseigha) for an order requiring the Metropolitan Police to disclose the evidence it had collected. Nigeria argued that it was in the public interest to do so. The police confirmed that it did not oppose the application, and, most important, the disclosure would not jeopardize further U.K. criminal investigations.

In November 2005, Nigeria's Economic and Financial Crimes Commission charged Mr. Alamieyeseigha criminally with 40 counts of money laundering and corruption. The case had an international dimension, with assets located in various jurisdictions such as the Bahamas, the British Virgin Islands, South Africa, Cyprus, Denmark, the United States, and the United Kingdom.

For the assets located in the United Kingdom, realizing that requesting mutual legal assistance in a criminal case would be time consuming and that orders from Nigerian courts would not necessarily be enforced, Nigeria brought civil proceedings in the United Kingdom High Court (Chancery Division) for summary judgment against two companies, Santolina Investment Corporation and Solomon & Peters Ltd., respectively incorporated in the Seychelles and the British Virgin Islands. Nigeria asked to recover real estate properties and funds officially held by the companies.

Both companies were controlled by Mr. Alamieyeseigha and used as corporate vehicles to hide assets allegedly derived from his corrupt conduct while governor of Bayelsa state. Mr. Alamieyeseigha was asserting that he had legitimate explanations for all of the assets claimed by Nigeria. In March 2007, on the first application for summary judgment, the U.K. judge gave a "reserved judgment," meaning that he refrained from taking an immediate decision and would take the matter under consideration.

In July 2007, in a separate criminal proceeding in Nigeria against the aforementioned companies and the former governor, Mr. Alamieyeseigha pleaded guilty to six charges of making false declaration of assets before the Federal High Court, and also pleaded guilty on behalf of Solomon & Peters and Santolina to charges of money laundering related to bribes paid to obtain government contracts. By pleading guilty and admitting his guilt in a court of law in Nigeria, he destroyed any possibility of mounting a reasonable defense against the suit. Accordingly, the Chancery Division of the London High Court used the new evidence of the guilty plea in Nigeria to allow a second hearing for summary judgment. This time the court granted summary judgment for Nigeria.

The court concluded that the bank balances and real estate investments held by the two companies controlled by Mr. Alamieyeseigha were derived from bribes and secret profits and should therefore be returned to the government of Nigeria as the legitimate owner of those assets. As a consequence, the court held that Nigeria was the true owner of three residential properties in London (registered under Solomon & Peters Ltd. as sole proprietor) and of the balances of certain bank accounts, amounting to approximately US$2.7 million (held at the Royal Bank of Scotland in the name of Santolina Investment Corporation) as well as US$1.5 million seized at the time of arrest. It turned out that Santolina was a corporate vehicle hiding assets related to offshore jurisdictions. The total amount recovered exceeded US$17.7 million.

2. Zambian Government v. the former Zambian President, Frederick Chiluba (United Kingdom)

Frederick Chiluba was president of Zambia from 1991 until 2002. After he left office, the Zambian authorities began a criminal investigation and also convened a task force on asset recovery. In February 2003, he was criminally charged in Zambia with 168 counts of misappropriation and laundering of more than US$40 million in state funds. The allegations involved assets that were diverted from the Ministry of Finance into an account held at the London branch of the Zambia National Commercial Bank (Zanaco). The Zambian government claimed that the account was used to meet Chiluba's personal expenses; the defendant argued that the account was used by Zambia's intelligence services to fund operations abroad.

In 2004, while the criminal case was pending in Zambia, the attorney general of Zambia filed a civil lawsuit in the United Kingdom on behalf of the people of Zambia. The claim was that Chiluba, together with former Zambian officials, had conspired with others fraudulently to misappropriate monies that belonged to Zambia. The venue was chosen largely because of the close nexus of assets and defendants with London, namely, (a) much of the allegedly stolen money was transferred through or held in accounts in London; (b) most of the funds diverted from Zambia had passed through law firms and bank accounts in the United Kingdom; (c) a number of individual defendants had close ties with London; and (d) finally, the judgments were easily and immediately enforceable without further legal action.

Mostly, Zambian authorities seized the opportunity to bring a private civil lawsuit in the United Kingdom because they believed it would offer the best hope of recovering some of the laundered money. To have seizure orders issued by English courts rather than Zambian courts would greatly increase the likelihood of enforceability of orders—also considering that the United Kingdom is party to the Brussels regime. The court in London found Chiluba and his codefendants liable in tort (misappropriation) for stealing US$46 million (£23 million).

In addition, the defendants were also adjudged to have breached their fiduciary duties owed to Zambia or to have dishonestly assisted in such breaches. The conspiracy was carried out by defendants' intimidating government employees and maintaining that there should be no challenge to what was going on because it was all "secret operations" of the government security arm, the ZSIS. Zambia prevailed and obtained several judgments. Zambia then enforced the judgments in different jurisdictions, recovering large sums. However, on the criminal side, Chiluba was eventually acquitted in Zambia.

Zambia also sought to establish the liability of two U.K. intermediaries in the corrupt schemes. Two English solicitors and their respective law firms (Iqbal Meer, of Meer Care & Desai, and Bimal Tacker, of Cave Malik) were sued for allegedly giving dishonest assistance in the misappropriation. The firms' bank accounts in London had allegedly been used in the payment of about $20 million by the Zambian government pursuant to an arms deal. The crucial issue was whether the lawyers had "crossed the line between being incompetent to being dishonest ('fool or knave' test)."

At the lower court level, the court found that the lawyer dishonestly assisted Chiluba and the Zambian defendants in their misconduct and had conspired to misappropriate monies from Zambia. The judge relied on the "constructive trust for dishonest assistance" theory. He considered that either the partner knew that the instructions he had carried out involved, in effect, handling stolen money, or he had had a clear suspicion that that was the case, which he chose to ignore (the "blind eye" definition). The court ordered Mr. Meer and the law firm to pay to Zambia more than US$11 million.

On appeal, however, the higher court reversed and decided that the two codefendant lawyers were not liable. The appellate court underlined that this was more a case of incompetence in understanding and carrying out professional duties than dishonest assistance to a corrupt scheme. Therefore, the lower court's order was dismissed. Nonetheless, the legal theory itself remained intact.

3. Kartika Ratna Thahir v. Pertamina (Singapore)

Pertamina Company is an Indonesian state-owned company created on September 15, 1971, by Law No. 8 of 1971, of the republic of Indonesia. Pertamina undertook major economic development projects at the direction of the Indonesian government. One of the main projects was the development of a huge industrial complex for steel-making and related industries. This project needed the contribution of external contractors to provide support. In that connection, two German companies, Siemens AG and Klockner Industrie Analegen Gmbh, entered the picture. Siemens provided the power generation equipment and Klockner built and equipped the water supply system.

M. Thahir was general assistant to the president director of Pertamina. His salary was about US$9,000 a year. At the date of his death, multiple Asian Currency Unit (ACU) deposits had been made on bank accounts in Singapore, denominated in their majority in deutschmarks (DM) and some in dollars. The bank accounts were opened under the name of M. Thahir and his wife.

The lower court found bribery. The court found that the money denominated in DM on M. Thahir's accounts in the Singaporean bank came from Siemens and Klockner and were bribes paid by these companies to M. Thahir to obtain more favorable contractual terms and preferential treatment. Pertamina sued to recover the bribes.

Pertamina learned about the bank accounts (held jointly by M. Thahir and his wife, Mrs. Kartika Ratna Thahir) after the death of M. Thahir, when a dispute had already arisen between his widow and his sons by an earlier marriage to recover these sums. Pertamina gave notice to the bank claiming to be entitled to the various deposits made to the account on the ground that they were wrongfully acquired by M. Thahir while being employed by Pertamina, and the acquisition was contrary to his duty as an employee of Pertamina.

The bank applied to the court for Pertamina to be joined as a defendant, alongside M. Thahir's widow and sons by an earlier marriage. The court had then to determine who was entitled to recover the monies deriving from bribes located on the Singaporean bank accounts.

The lower court accepted the claim of Pertamina, emphasizing that in view of the far-reaching extent of M. Thahir's duties and responsibilities, "it is difficult to envisage any clearer situation giving rise to a fiduciary relationship." Indeed, the courts found that Thahir owed a fiduciary duty to Pertamina Company and that the bribes received by him were held as a constructive trustee for it, meaning the company held a proprietary claim to the funds.

M. Thahir's widow appealed this decision, arguing that Pertamina knew about and consented to the bribes and consequently was not able to have a proprietary claim on the

ACU deposits. The appellate court dismissed her claim, stating that she did not produce a shred of evidence to show that Pertamina had knowledge of or had given consent to the receipt by M. Thahir of the sums.

The appellate court agreed with the judge of first instance and stated that "the appellant (M. Thahir's widow) knowingly assisted M. Thahir in his dishonest and fraudulent design to receive the bribes represented by the deposits, and, in addition, she also received the trust property, i.e. the deposits, when she became the sole legal owner thereof on the death of her husband. Accordingly, at all material times, she held the deposits on trust for Pertamina."

4. Federal Republic of Nigeria v. Joshua Dariye & Another (United Kingdom)

From May 1999 to May 2007, Joshua Dariye was the governor of Plateau state in the federal republic of Nigeria. During his administration, Dariye allegedly misappropriated more than US$11.9 million. Nigeria learned that some of these funds were used to purchase property in London, and some were funneled into bank accounts in the United Kingdom and Nigeria.

In 2005 and 2007, in the courts of the United Kingdom, Nigeria initiated two civil actions to confiscate Dariye's ill-gotten assets. Eventually, Nigeria successfully obtained judgment in both cases. Dariye tried to challenge the jurisdiction of the U.K. court, arguing that Nigeria was a more appropriate forum. The court rejected Dariye's challenge for three main reasons: (a) Dariye's motion appeared to be a delaying tactic rather than a good faith challenge; (b) the location of the main witnesses in Nigeria was not an obstacle to the trial to be held in the United Kingdom; and (c) the enforcement of the judgment would be easier if it was obtained directly in the United Kingdom.

The court examined whether it would be difficult to enforce a judgment obtained in Nigeria in relation to bank accounts found in England and took into account that a Nigerian court would have problems obtaining disclosure from English banks. The court therefore decided that the United Kingdom was the proper forum. During the litigation, Nigeria was able to get an order from the U.K. court ordering disclosure to Nigeria of information gathered during a criminal investigation by U.K. authorities, when the authorities did not oppose and affirmed that disclosure would not prejudice their investigations.

5. JSC BTA Bank v. Ablyazov & Others (United Kingdom)

Mr. Ablyazov was the chairman of the Kazakh Bank BTA, in Kazakhstan. After he left the bank, in 2009, large sums were found to be missing from BTA's accounts.

Mr. Ablyazov was accused of embezzlement on a vast scale and misappropriation of the assets of the bank. He fled to the United Kingdom and successfully claimed asylum. However, BTA, which became owned by the Kazakh state investment fund, sued him in the United Kingdom before the London High Court, demanding US$6 billion back and claiming that Mr. Ablyavoz had funneled embezzled money into buying multiple properties and investments in the United Kingdom and around the world. BTA bank sought a freeze of the assets. At an early stage in the proceedings in conjunction with the freeze order, Mr. Ablyazov was required to provide full disclosure of his assets.

Mr. Ablyazov appealed this order, claiming his privilege against self-incrimination, in particular that compliance with the order might lead him to disclose information that could be used against him in criminal proceedings in Kazakhstan. Mr. Ablyazov's appeal was dismissed for a variety of reasons, although BTA agreed in this case that the disclosure would be initially confined to the claimants' solicitors and counsel, with the issue of wider disclosure to be resolved at a later date. Eventually, during the court hearing, BTA successfully argued that Mr. Ablyazov was continuing to move his money around despite being ordered not to, and the court found him guilty of contempt of court, sentencing him in February 2012 to 22 months' imprisonment.

Since Mr. Ablyazov was moving his assets notwithstanding the court order, BTA next applied for a receivership order. The court had to balance the risk of asset dissipation and the property rights of Mr. Ablyazov. BTA supported its request for a receiver with two main arguments: (a) that the defendant was using structures based on nominees who acted for him and using corporate structures in jurisdictions "renowned for their secrecy and light regulation"; and (b) that he had continuously breached the freezing order. The court concluded that it was necessary to appoint a receiver in support of the freezing order to preserve assets and prevent their dissipation prior to trial. The receivership order was designed to enable the receivers to assume control of the corporate structures used.

6. Attorney General of Turks and Caicos Islands v. Star Platinum Island Ltd. et al.

Star Platinum and related companies sought to develop a resort in the Turks and Caicos Islands. Using several intermediary vehicles, in 2007 principals of Star Platinum made a payment of US$500,000 to the then-chief minister, Michael Misick. A short time later, the government of Turks and Caicos Islands granted Star Platinum favorable terms for long-term leases for additional property that would enhance the value of the project: For instance, the company paid $3.2 million for the leases, which was a small fraction of their market value. Furthermore, the company was also granted three separate leases over a combined area of more than 500 acres, with option to purchase the majority of that land (again at prices far lower than the official market value), and a development agreement that provided Star Platinum with the right to undertake development projects on the lands.

In the Turks and Caicos court, the attorney general sued Star Platinum, alleging civil bribery, namely, that the money paid to the chief minister had been a bribe, and demanding to rescind the leases. The defendants argued that the payment was not a bribe but a political donation to the political party that had been in power at that time.

In June 2013, the court found a very strong probability that the $500,000 was a bribe and that the leases were the result of the bribe payment. The court ruled that the attorney general was entitled to rescind the transfer and to recover either the amount of the bribe or damages resulting from the bribe (but not both). The judge also found that Star Platinum was liable for damages arising out of the breaches of the development agreement and that the leases entered into pursuant to the development agreement had been determined upon its termination.

Regarding the effect of the rescission of the contract, the court found that the state was not required to repay the $3.2 million that Star Platinum had paid under the tainted lease deal, since a bank had acquired bona fide rights in the property as security for the principal's debts: the bank had taken a charge of the property to secure repayment of the $3.2 million. The court estimated that Star Platinum had not been enriched by the rescission, since the value of the property had been reduced because of the charge.

Consequently, the court was satisfied that the damages that Star Platinum was liable to pay to the attorney general were comfortably in excess of the remaining amount that would be payable on a restitution basis. The court therefore ordered that the transfer be set aside without any payment being required from the attorney general.

Appendix C. Table of Cases Mentioned

1. Core of text

Case law	Chapter	XPage
Box 1.1 - Ferdinand Marcos Case - Dec. 1, 1988 (United States)	Chapter 1 (A) (2)	15
Box 1.2 - The Republic of Iraq v. ABB AG et al. – Feb. 6, 2013 (United States)	Chapter 1 (A) (2)	15
Box 1.3 - Nigeria v. Santolina Investment Corporation, Diepreye Alamieyeseigha and Others – Dec. 3, 2007 (United Kingdom)	Chapter 1 (A) (2)	16
Box 1.4 - Republic of Brazil v. Durant, JRC [Isle of Jersey] 211 (2012) Maluf Case in Jersey – Nov. 16, 2012 (Isle of Jersey)	Chapter 1 (A) (2)	17
Box 1.5 - Kartika Ratna Thahir v. Pertamina – August 25, 1994 (Singapore)	Chapter 1 (A) (2)	18
Box 1.6 - Tunisia as partie civile in context of criminal cases involving asset recovery	Chapter 1 (A) (3)	18
Box 1.7 - Claims under property law to compensate victims of corruption: the example of the State of Bosnia and Herzegovina	Chapter 1 (A) (3)	19
Box 1.8 - Continental Management v. United States – Dec. 17, 1975 (United States)	Chapter 1 (B) (1)	21
Box 1.9 - Attorney General of Zambia v. Meer Care & Desai (a firm) & Ors., [2007] EWHC 952 (Ch) – May 4, 2007 (United Kingdom)	Chapter 1 (B) (2)	22
Box 3.1 - Federal Republic of Nigeria v. Joshua Dariye & Another – March 12, 2007 (United Kingdom)	Chapter 3 (A)	40
Box 3.2 - Attorney General of Zambia v. Meer Care & Desai (a firm) & Ors., [2007] EWHC 952 (Ch) – May 4, 2007 (United Kingdom)	Chapter 3 (A)	43
Box 3.3 - Ukrvaktsina v. Olden Group, LLC, Case No. 6:10-cv-06297-AA (D. Ore.) – Oct. 30, 2011 (United States)	Chapter 3 (A)	44
Box 3.4 - Alba v. Alcoa Company – Settlement with U.S. government – Announced Jan. 9, 2014 (United States)	Chapter 3 (A)	45
Box 3.5 - Fiona Trust & Holding Corp. & Ors. v. Dimitri Skarga & Ors. [2013] EWCA Civ 275 – March 26, 2013 (United Kingdom)	Chapter 3 (B)	46
Box 4.1 - State of Libya v. Capitana Seas Ltd. – March 9, 2012 (United Kingdom)	Chapter 4 (A) (1)	51
Box 4.2 - Nigeria v. Santolina Investment Corporation, Diepreye Alamieyeseigha & Others - Dec. 3, 2007 (United Kingdom)	Chapter 4 (A) (1)	52
Box 4.3 - AG of Hong Kong v. Reid – Nov. 1, 1993 (Hong Kong)	Chapter 4 (A) (1)	53

(continued next page)

(continued next page)

Case law	Chapter	XPage
Box 7.2 - Case City of Cannes – Cour d'appel (Dec. 14, 2005) and Cour de cassation – March 14, 2007 (France)	Chapter 7 (A) (1)	92
Box 7.3 - S.T. Grand Inc. v. City of New York – April 11, 1972 (United States)	Chapter 7 (A) (2)	92
Box 7.4 - Cameroon Airlines v. Transnet Ltd. [2004] APP.L.R. 07/29 – July 29, 2004 (United Kingdom)	Chapter 7 (A) (2)	93
Box 7.6 - County of San Bernardino v. Walsh 158 Cal.App.4th 533, 69 Cal. Rptr. 3d 848 (Cal. App. 2 Dist. 2007) – Dec. 27, 2007 (United States)	Chapter 7 (B)	96
Box 8.1 - Attorney General of Zambia v. Meer Care & Desai (a firm) & Ors., [2007] EWHC 952 (Ch) (United Kingdom)	Chapter 8 (A) (1)	103
Box 8.2 - Swiss Federal Supreme Court (4A_366/2011) – Oct. 31, 2011 (Switzerland)	Chapter 8 (A) (2)	104
Box 8.3 - Federal Republic of Nigeria v. Joshua Dariye & Another – March 12, 2007 (United Kingdom)	Chapter 8 (A) (3)	106
Box 8.4 - Kuwaiti Investment Organization / Sheikh Fahad Mohammed al-Sabah – Civil judgment in 1999 in U.K. (United Kingdom)	Chapter 8 (A) (3)	106
Box 9.2 - JSC BTA Bank v. Ablyazov & Others – Oct. 27, 2009 (United Kingdom)	Chapter 9 (B)	113

2. Cases mentioned in footnotes

XFootnote number	Case law	Chapter	XPage
1	Attorney General for Hong Kong v. Reid [1994] 1 Ac 324 at 330-1 – Nov. 1, 1993 (Hong Kong SAR, China)	Intro	1
6	Siemens Telecom and Other Sectors Cases	Intro	4
1	Korea Supply Co. v. Lockheed Martin Corp., 29 Cal. 4th 1134, 63 P.3d 937 (Cal. 2003) (United States)	Chapter 1	11
2	SNC- Lavalin civil suits (Canada)	Chapter 1	11
a.	London High Court of Justice, Diepreye Solomon Peter Alamieyeseigha v. The Crown Prosecution Services, Case No.: CO/9133/2005 – Nov. 25, 2005 (United Kingdom)	Chapter 1 (A) (3)	16
b.	Federal High Court of Nigeria, Lagos, Federal Republic of Nigeria v. Diepreye Alamieyeseigha & Ors., Suit No. FHC/U328C/05 (Nigeria)	Chapter 1 (A) (3)	16

(continued next page)

XFootnote number	Case law	Chapter	XPage
	Federal Criminal Court, Cour des Plaintes, A. v. Republic of Tunisia and Ministere Public de la Confederation – March 20, 2012 (Switzerland)	Chapter 1 (A) (3)	18
13	Tribunal de Grande Instance de Paris, 11th chamber, Case against Dan Etété – Nov. 7, 2007 (France)	Chapter 1 (A) (3)	18
	State of Bosnia and Herzegovina v. Momcilo Mandic et al. (first instance: 27 October 2006) KPV 02/06; Confirmed on appeal KPV 03/07 (March 29 2007)	Chapter 1 (A) (3)	19
9	Supreme Court (USA) Piper Aircraft v. Reyno, 454 U.S. 235, 250 – Dec. 8, 1981 (United States)	Chapter 3 (A)	44
2	Foskett v. McKeown and others [2001] 1 A.C. 102 (H.L.) (England)	Chapter 4 (A) (1)	50
c.	London High Court of Justice, Diepreye Solomon Peter Alamieyeseigha v. The Crown Prosecution Services, Case No.: CO/9133/2005 – Nov. 25, 2005 (United Kingdom)	Chapter 4 (A) (1)	52
c.	Nigeria v. Santolina Investment Corp. and Ors., [2007] EWHC 3053 (Q.B.) – March 7, 2007 (United Kingdom)		
a.	Royal Court of Jersey – Lloyds Trust Company (Channel Island) Ltd. v. The Government of Mozambique and Others – Oct. 31, 2013 (Isle of Jersey)	Chapter 4 (A) (1)	54
8	Ross River Ltd. v. Cambridge City Football Club Ltd. [2007] EWHC 2115 (Ch) – Sept. 19, 2007 (United Kingdom)	Chapter 4 (B) (1)	57
13	Wrotham Park Estate Co. Ltd. v. Parkside Homes Ltd. [1974] 1 WLR 798 – Jan. 1, 1974 (United Kingdom)	Chapter 4 (B) (1)	59
20	Industries & General Mortgage Co. Ltd. v. Lewis [1949] 2 All ER 573 (United Kingdom)	Chapter 4 (B) (2)	63
27	Cour de Cassation, Civ. 2eme, 10 mai 2012, n 11-14.739 (France)	Chapter 4 (B) (4)	66
28	Lamb v. Phillip Morris, 915 F. 2d 1024, 1027-30 (6th Cir.) – Sept. 28, 1990 (United States)	Chapter 4 (B) (4)	66
	J.S. Service Center Corp. and Sercenco, S.A. v. General Technical Services Co., Inc. and General Electric Company – July 17, 1996 (United States)		
30	Glazer Capital Mgmt. LP v. Magistri, 549 F.3d 736 (9th Cir.) – Nov. 26. 2008 (United States)	Chapter 4 (B) (4)	66

(continued next page)

XFootnote number	Case law	Chapter	XPage
31	Dooley v. United Technologies Corp., 803 F.Supp. 428 (D.D.C. 1992) – June 17, 1992 (United States)	Chapter 4 (B) (4)	66
	Environmental Tectonics v. W.S. Kirkpatrick Inc., 847 F.2d 1052 (3d Cir. 1988) – May 2, 1988 (United States)		
34	United States v. Balsys, 525 U.S. 666, 669 – June 25, 1998 (United States)	Chapter 4 (B) (4)	68
1	Bankers Trust v. Shapira [1980] 1WLR 1274 – June 4, 1980 (United Kingdom)	Chapter 5 (A) (1)	72
2	Bank Mellat v. Nikpour [1985] FSR 87 (CA) (United Kingdom)	Chapter 5 (A) (2)	72
10	Bishopsgate Investment Management Ltd. v. Maxwell (No. 2) [1993] BCLC 814 – Feb. 16, 1993 (United Kingdom)	Chapter 5 (A) (4)	75

Appendix D. Resources

1. Website Resources

International Organizations and Bodies

World Bank Group

- World Bank: http://www.worldbank.org
- Financial Market Integrity Group: http://www.worldbank.org/amlcft

Stolen Asset Recovery (StAR) Initiative

- StAR: http://www.worldbank.org/star

United Nations

- United Nations: http://www.un.org
- United Nations Office on Drugs and Crime: http://www.unodc.org
- United Nations Convention against Corruption (UNCAC): http://www.unodc
  .org/unodc/en/treaties/CAC/index.html
- United Nations Convention against the Illicit Traffic in Narcotic Drugs and
  Psychotropic Substances, 1988: http://www.unodc.org/unodc/en/treaties/illicit
  -trafficking.html
- United Nations Convention against Transnational Organized Crime (UNTOC):
  http://www.unodc.org/unodc/en/treaties/CTOC/index.html

Organization for Economic Co-operation and Development Convention on Combating
Bribery of Foreign Public Officials in International Business Transactions: http://www
.oecd.org/document/20/0,3343,en_2649_34859_2017813_1_1_1_1,00.html

Inter-American Convention against Corruption: http://www.oas.org/juridico/english
/treaties/b-58.html

Council of Europe Conventions and Groups: http://conventions.coe.int

- Civil Law Convention on Corruption, 4 November 1999, at http://conventions
  .coe.int/treaty/en/Treaties/Html/174.htm
- GRECO Group of States against Corruption, at http://www.coe.int/t/dghl
  /monitoring/greco/default_en.asp

Decisions and Regulations from the Council of the European Union: http://eur-lex
.europa.eu

African Union Convention on Preventing and Combating Corruption, 2003: http://
www.au.int/en/sites/default/files/AFRICAN_UNION_CONVENTION
_PREVENTING_COMBATING_CORRUPTION.pdf

Commonwealth of Independent States Convention on Legal Assistance and Legal
Relations in Civil, Family and Criminal Matters: http://www.hcch.net/upload/wop
/jdgm_info01e.pdf

Financial Action Task Force (FATF) on Money Laundering: http://www.fatf-gafi.org

Organizations, Rating Agencies, and Bar Associations That Track Asset Recovery Attorneys

International Chamber of Commerce, at http://www.iccwbo.org/

U4, The Anti-Corruption Resource Centre, at http://www.u4.no/

FraudNet, at http://www.icc-ccs.org/home/fraudnet

The World Bank International Corruption Hunters, at http://web.worldbank.org
/WBSITE/EXTERNAL/EXTABOUTUS/ORGANIZATION/ORGUNITS/EXTDOII
/0,,contentMDK:23195265~menuPK:588927~pagePK:64168445~piPK:64168309~t
heSitePK:588921,00.html

Chambers and Partners, at www.chambersandpartners.com/

Online Sources for Case Law

StAR Corruption Cases DataBase: http://star.worldbank.org/corruption-cases/?db=All

British and Irish Legal Information Institute (BAILII): www.bailii.org/

French legal framework and case laws (Legifrance): www.legifrance.gouv.fr/

Asset Recovery Knowledge Center, at http://www.assetrecovery.org/

2. Publications and Studies

World Bank and StAR Publications (all available online at http://star.worldbank
.org)

Jean-Pierre Brun, Clive Scott, Kevin M. Stephenson, and Larissa Gray, *Asset Recovery
Handbook: A Guide for Practitioners*, World Bank Publications, 2011.

Emile van der Does de Willebois, Emily M. Halter, Robert A. Harrison, Ji Won
Park, and J. C. Sharman, *The Puppet Masters—How the Corrupt Use Legal
Structures to Hide Stolen Assets and What to Do about It*, World Bank Publications,
2011.

Theodore S. Greenberg, Linda M. Samuel, Wingate Grant, and Larissa Gray, *A Good
Practices Guide for Non-conviction Based Asset Forfeiture*, World Bank Publications,
2009.

Jacinta Oduor, Jeanne Hauch, Marianne Mathias, Ji Won Park, Oliver Stolpe, Agustin
Flah, and Dorothee Gottwald, *Left Out of the Bargain: Settlements in Foreign Bribery
Cases and Implications for Asset Recovery*, World Bank Publications, 2013.

OECD/StAR, *Identification and Quantification of the Proceeds of Bribery: A Joint OECD -StAR Analysis*, 2011.

OECD/StAR, *Tracking Anti-Corruption and Asset Recovery Commitments*, 2011.

Kevin M. Stephenson, Larissa Gray, Ric Power, Jean-Pierre Brun, Gabriele Dunker, and Melissa Panjer, *Barriers to Asset Recovery: An Analysis of the Key Barriers and Recommendations for Action*, World Bank Publications, 2011.

Books

Sir William Blackstone, *Commentaries of the Laws of England—Of the Nature of Crimes and Their Punishment* (Book 4, Chapter 1), Oxford University Press (1765–69), available online at http://www.lonang.com/exlibris/blackstone/bla-401.htm.

Shelby R. Grubbs, *International Civil Procedure (World Law Group Series)*, Kluwer Law International, 2003.

Donald Harris, David Campbell, and Roger Halson, *Remedies in Contract and Tort*, 2nd ed., Cambridge University Press, 2005.

Gunter Heine, Barbara Huber, and Thomas O. Rose, *Private Commercial Bribery*, ICC, 2003.

Anne Héritier Lachat (ed.) and Ursula Cassani (ed.), *Lutte Contre La Corruption— The Never-ending Story*, Schulthess Verlag, Zürich, 2011.

Bernd H. Klose (ed.), *Asset Tracing and Recovery—The FraudNet World Compendium*, ICC FraudNet, Erich Schmidt Verlag, 2010.

Olaf Meyer (ed.), *The Civil Law Consequences of Corruption*, Nomos, 2009.

Colin Nicholls QC, Tim Daniel, Alan Bacarese, and John Hatchard, *Corruption and Misuse of Public Office*, 2nd ed., Oxford University Press, 2011.

Articles and Working Papers Available Online

Commission of the European Communities, "*Commission Staff Working Paper, Accompanying the White Paper on Damages Actions for Breach of the EC Antitrust Rules*," 2008, available at http://eur-lex.europa.eu/LexUriServ/LexUriServ .do?uri=SEC:2008:0404:FIN:EN:PDF.

Council of Europe, *Civil Forfeiture (confiscation in rem): Explanatory and Impact Study*, Technical paper prepared by Arvinder Sambei, 2012, available at http://www.coe .int/t/dghl/cooperation/economiccrime/corruption/projects/car_serbia /Technical%20papers/2358%20CAR%20-%20TP%2020%20-%20Arvinder%20 Sambei%20-%20Impact%20Study%20on%20Civil%20Forfeiture%20-%20May%20 2012%20-%20ENG%20(2).pdf.

Leonard L. Gumport, *Public Corruption-Maximizing Remedies*, County Counsels' Association of California, 2005 Annual Meeting Conference, 2005, available at http://www.grlegal.com/Articles/public_corruption_mem_7-11-06.pdf.

Martin S. Kenney, *Mareva by Letter—Preserving Assets Extra-Judicially, Destroying a Bank's Defense of Good Faith by Exposing It to Actual Knowledge of Fraud*, FraudNet Meeting, 2006, available at http://icc-ccs.org/home/publications /viewdownload/3/22.

Markus Löffelmann, *The Victim in Criminal Proceedings: A Systematic Portrayal of Victim Protection under German Criminal Procedure Law*, from Resource Material Series N° 70, pp. 41–68, Simon Cornell, ed., 2006, available at http://www.unafei.or .jp/english/pdf/RS_No70/No70_06VE_Loffelmann1.pdf.

Juanita Olaya, Kodjo Attisso, and Anja Roth, *Repairing Social Damage out of Corruption Cases: Opportunities and Challenges as Illustrated in the Alcatel Case in Costa Rica*, International Anti-Corruption Conference, 2010, available at http://14iacc.org/wp -content/uploads/SocialDamagePaper20.01.2011.pdf.

Joseph R. Profaizer (Wilmer, Cutler & Pickering), *Effective Use of Legal and Asset-tracing Remedies for Corruption: Civil Legal Remedies*, paper prepared for the 9th International Anti-Corruption Conference, 1999, available at http://9iacc.org /papers/day3/ws1/d3ws1_jrprofaizer.html.

Susan Rose-Ackerman and Paul D. Carrington, *Anti-Corruption Policy: Can International Actors Play a Constructive Role?*, Carolina Academic Press, Durham, NC, 2013, available at http://graduateinstitute.ch/files/live/sites/iheid/files/sites/ctei/shared /CTEI/Pauwelyn/Publications/rose-ackerman-carrington%20pdf%20(2).pdf.

Douglas R. Young (Farella Braun & Martel LLP), *The Foreign Corrupt Practices Act as a Factor in Private Civil Litigation*, 2002, available at http://www.fbm.com/files/Publica tion/2b79d8bf-740f-45c7-8ff2-9980da7c7b89/Presentation/PublicationAttachment /e70b13d2-ecca-4bf3-807d-99b19fd76632/3C02CACD-4C60-467B-B371-5C58427 333E0_document.pdf.

Simon N. M. Young, "Why Civil Actions against Corruption?" *Journal of Financial Crime* 16, no. 2 (2009), available at http://www.emeraldinsight.com/journals.htm? articleid=1789998.

Other Academic Articles

Robert J. Augustine, "Obtaining International Judicial Assistance under the Federal Rules and the Hague Convention on the Taking of Evidence Abroad in Civil and Commercial Matters," *Georgia Journal of International and Comparative Law*, vol. 10 (1980): 101.

James Maton and Tim Daniel, "Recovering the Proceeds of Corruption by Public Officials: A Case Study," *Academy of European Law*, vol. 10, no. 3 (2009): 453–65.

www.ingramcontent.com/pod-product-compliance
Lightning Source LLC
Chambersburg PA
CBHW082357270326
41935CB00013B/1656